Now is the tim...
self, full of hope and freedom.

GENUINE IMITATION

JOHN MASON

Genuine Imitation

Published by Insight International, Inc.
contact@freshword.com
www.freshword.com
918-493-1718

ISBN: 978-1-943361-35-9
E-Book ISBN: 978-1-943361-36-6

Library of Congress Control Number: 2017901862

Printed in the United States of America.

DEDICATION

I am proud to dedicate this book to my beautiful wife, Linda, our four great kids—Michelle, Greg, Mike, and Dave, my two daughters-in-law, Brittany and Kelley, and my three grandchildren, Emma, Olivia, and Beckett.

To Linda, for your prayers and love.

To Michelle, for your dedication and unwavering commitment to excellence.

To Greg, for your peaceful faith and support.

To Mike, for your creativity and worshipful heart.

To Dave, for your competitive spirit and "Dave and Dad" fun.

To Brittany and Kelley, for your love for my sons and your love for the Lord.

To Emma, Olivia, and Beckett, for the sweetness, laughter, and abundance of love you've brought to our entire family.

Your support, help, encouragement, sense of humor, and prayers sustain and bless me every day.

CONTENTS

PART I

Your Authentic Self

1 Genuine or Imitation?

I've never liked dressing up. Especially under the onus of a theme. Dress like a cowboy for this party, be a celebrity for this gathering, wear clothes from the sixties for this celebration. Some people love this, but I don't. In fact, there have been several times where I was excited to get the invitation only to discover I had to be a farm animal or some other uncomfortable thing. So I just don't go.

I'm not saying that dressing up in some outrageous outfit is wrong. Far from it. It's just when our whole lives are one costume, conversation, or action that's not genuine that drives me crazy. Too many people are "dressed up" in something other than themselves and spend their whole lives that way.

Wanting to be myself has been in me since I was born into this world back in the mid-fifties. I like my genuine self, and I prefer others that way too. I think God also does. The Bible says in 1 Corinthians 12 that it pleased Him how He made us. God made you and me exactly as He wanted, yet there's still room for improvement.

Imagine God with a great big smile on His face the day you were born. And smiling even wider every time you're genuinely being *you*. For some reason, that's easy for me to picture.

While working at a publishing company, we decided to create a Bible. Not write one, but create one using the King James Version (the version the disciples used...just kidding). It would include commentary from all our prominent authors.

In collecting samples to study, I came across a Bible with the words "Genuine Imitation Leather" stamped in gold foil on its back cover. I immediately thought that was a funny saying, maybe like the expression "jumbo shrimp," which also makes me laugh.

Sometimes this kind of "leather" is called pleather. It looks like the real thing, but it's fake and plastic. Whether that bothers you is based on your opinion of leather. And that's my point: we should all value what God values...our genuine selves.

As I looked at the Genuine Imitation Leather imprint, I thought, *A lot of us Christians are like this. Genuine, but living an imitation life. Sincere, but not ourselves. Dedicated, but not free. Doing the best we can, but full of regrets.* Like this Bible packaging, we want to appear to be something respected and valuable, but we're an imitation of what we think people want us to be.

How do we get here? We don't start out that way. If there's genuine *anything* in the world, it's a baby. We start out completely real and honest.

From infancy through the start of school, we're generally thinking, *Why not?* Anything is possible. Kids are genuine because they are always asking questions and are open to viewing the world from many viewpoints: the sports hero, the superhero, the prince or princess, the clown, the mommy or daddy, and others.

They are always creating stories or imagining different ways to use ordinary things, like making drums out of household items or a hat from nearly anything. What they feel from the inside, they do. This is what my grandchildren do every day.

I believe there's something inside of every person crying out to be who God created them to be. Not a job title, a status level, or a physical achievement—but that person you know you genuinely are.

The purpose behind everything I write in this book is to bring you hope, freedom, and encouragement.

Many of the stories I'm going to tell you happened a number of years ago. There's a reason for that—I think sometimes only the perspective of time can help us fully understand what God was doing in those earlier moments.

It's fascinating to see how God in every single case found a way, a way that only He can, to turn what looked bad into something good. Everything does work together for good for those who love Him and are called according to His purpose (see Romans 8:28).

My hope is, as I share with you some of the stories that happened to me, that you will avoid trouble and, more importantly, understand that God is at work in your life. Sometimes you won't see it until later. He's already in your future, He's working on your behalf, and He is for you.

It's not too late to be your authentic self, full of hope and freedom.

2 You're Peculiar, So Don't Change.

Once during the late 1980s, I was up early reading the morning paper, the *Tulsa World.* It was a daily ritual I'm sure I learned from my dad. Nowadays, if you see someone reading an actual newspaper, it's almost certain they're over forty.

This day there was an article from the Associated Press that caught my eye. The report stated, "Here's the average American." The piece began to describe in some detail the "average" American. They make x number of dollars a year… I thought, *That's what I'm making.* This Average American lives in this kind of house worth x. *Hey, that's how much my house is worth.*

The Average American has two children. Yes, at that time we had two kids. *Wow, this is getting interesting*, I thought.

The article went on to say that the most common name for a man is…wait for it…John! And the most common name for a woman is…drumroll…Linda! *Yes, that's my wife's name!*

I was amazed. I didn't know what to think. *Is this good?* I thought. *Or not so good?* Then I began to get a little upset—then a bit more upset. I had just been declared the most average person in America. (At least that's how it felt.)

I said out loud, "I'm not average! And you're not going to tell me I am." I don't care what the numbers say or what a respected news organization says, or what anyone says. *I am not average*, I thought resolutely. God fearfully and wonderfully made me to be unique.

At that moment, the seeds for my first book, *An Enemy Called Average*, were planted. My passion for telling others that they, too, are not average, rose inside me.

Never let others, no matter what the "facts" may say, tell you that you're average. You are a genuine, one-of-a-kind, break-the-mold person.

You are unique. No one who has ever been before or who will come after is like you.

You may not think that the world needs you, but it does. God planned it that way.

No one can speak with your voice, say your words, smile your smile, or shine your light. No one can take your place, for it is yours alone to fill.

If you are not here to shine your light, who knows how many other people will lose their way as they pass by your empty place in the world. You can brighten the world by leaving a little of your sparkle everywhere you go.

There are people connected to you who are waiting to be impacted by you. You may be the answer to their prayer. A solution to their problem. An answer to their question.

Out of one hundred billion galaxies and one hundred billion star systems, you're one out of seven billion people. You have your own genetic makeup, and your thumbprint is like none other. You are as unique as every cloud formation in the sky and as every falling snowflake. Being this unique is so much better than being perfect.

Someone will always be prettier. Someone will always be smarter. Someone will always be younger. Someone will always be richer. But they will never be you.

Be yourself and live the story that no one else can live—the story of your own unique life.

3

You Are One Decision Away from a Totally Different Life.

—Mark Batterson

We have no right to complain about what we permit. Some of our troubles continue because we allow them.

I had just begun to travel and speak in churches when I received an invitation from a church in Buffalo, New York. The pastor was a wonderful man who had a church in downtown Buffalo, along with connections to other churches in the area. He arranged for me to speak in his church and in several others while I was there.

I was new at all of this, so I pretty much accepted whatever arrangements people set up for me. On the phone before I arrived, the pastor told me that one of his essential prerequisites for all traveling ministers was that they stay in his house and fellowship with some of his church members.

He picked me up at the airport and drove me straight to his house, where a group of about a dozen church members greeted us. We had a wonderful dinner together and spent several hours talking and sharing about how good the Lord had been in each of our lives.

When I'd first arrived, the pastor had told me to put my luggage in a bedroom down the hallway from where dinner was being served. I noticed a small bed in the room, but didn't think much of it.

As the dinner concluded and everybody left, the pastor directed me back to that same room and told me that we would have breakfast at the house in the morning and then go over to the church.

The door behind me closed. I stood alone in the room…looking at the smallest bed I have ever seen. I wondered if he was joking with me or trying to pull a prank.

The bed was maybe half the size of a twin bed. I laid on it with my feet hanging off the end—and I'm only five foot eight inches tall. I barely fit on the bed. There was absolutely no room to turn right or left without landing on the floor. I was about to sleep at attention all night!

I didn't sleep very well and kept dreaming about falling off a cliff, to my right and then to my left, all night long. I woke up the next morning thankful I was alive, ate breakfast, and preached the best sermon I could.

I decided from that point forward I was only going to sleep at a hotel with regular beds and never again in someone's house.

I never figured out why he put me in that room with that bed. But I took away these lessons, straight from the Bible: you have not because you ask not, and ask and you will receive.

Successful people make decisions based on where they want to be. Decide something today that your future self will thank you for.

Being decisive is not easy. Sometimes the hardest thing and the right thing are the same.

Too many of us lose hope or feel less free, simply because we allow it. We all need to be more decisive.

The road of life is paved with flat squirrels who ran into the middle of the road, then couldn't decide which way to go. You're not a product of your circumstances, but rather your decisions. Results and success follow commitment and decisions.

Do you say this? "I used to be indecisive, but now I'm not sure."

"There comes a day when you realize turning the page is the best feeling in the world because you realize there is so much more to the book than the page you were stuck on" (Zayn Malik).

One day you'll wake up and you'll be so glad you didn't settle for just anything. You chose God's plan.

Don't settle for the "short bed" your whole life. "In the end, we only regret the chances we didn't take, relationships we were afraid to have, and the decisions we waited too long to make" (Lewis Carroll).

4 Mr. President, Are You Recording Our Conversation?

When I was seventeen years old, I was honored to be selected as part of a group called the Youth Report to the President. It was 1973, and twelve young people were chosen from around the country to personally meet with the president.

Of course, I remember that moment quite vividly. First, the Oval Office is, well, oval. There's the seal of the president in the middle of the room's carpet, the president's desk backs up to the Rose Garden, and it's all quite impressive, as you can imagine.

I stood right next to President Nixon the whole meeting. I remember him as a couple of inches taller than me and thinking, *This is the most powerful man in the world.* Also, I must admit I thought, *He's got the biggest nose I've ever seen, just like the cartoons depict.* Only a teenager would think that...

There were lots of rules for us while we were there. Of course, we were not allowed to ask the president any questions, but he could ask us questions.

There were plenty of Secret Service people and media there with us. Both were watching our every move, it seemed. Before we met the president, we were taken to places the general public couldn't go, such as the floor where the first family lived and into the room where Franklin Roosevelt gave his fireside chats.

Henry Kissinger dropped by, as did John Ehrlichman and H.R. Haldeman (of later Watergate fame). It was a very heady experience, but honestly, it was mostly a photo opportunity for the president. Remember "the generation gap"? Well, I supposed this meeting made him look like he was bridging that gap.

About nine months earlier, my father had taken me to see Richard Nixon when he was campaigning in the city where I grew up, Fort Wayne, Indiana.

It was at this campaign event that my dad noticed Richard Nixon's press secretary, Ron Zigler, out in the crowd. He approached Mr. Zigler to say hello and introduce me. At that moment, Mr. Zigler asked us if we would like a gift from the president. Of course we said yes. He promptly gave us a nice tie clasp with the seal of the president and the president's signature on it.

So I'm meeting with President Nixon, and I'm wearing the tie clasp. At the end of our meeting, he asked us if we would like a gift. Of course we all said yes, and he began to go down the row giving each person a gift.

When he came to me, he reached out to give me a tie clasp (the same one I was wearing). I told him I already had one. He began to laugh and asked me how. So, I told him the Ron Zigler story. He immediately had his aide get me another gift, which was a beautiful set of cufflinks with the presidential seal. I still have both today. Interestingly, a large picture of Richard Nixon and me laughing together ended up on the front page of the *Washington Star* newspaper that next morning.

As a result of meeting with the president, I am on the Watergate tapes. Here's how I found out.

About a year after I was in Richard Nixon's office, an article in *Newsweek* magazine appeared describing people who were recorded while in the Oval Office with Richard Nixon. Our group, the Youth Report to the President, was mentioned as one of those groups. And that's how I ended up on the Watergate tapes.

When I find myself in an unusual place, I'm on the lookout for what God might be up to. It's a holy suspicion that He's at work in my life and in the lives of the others I'm around.

God is like that. He places you places. Then He does more than we can ask or think.

I've heard it said that God likes to play hide-and-seek with us. He wants us to seek Him with our whole heart. The Bible encourages us, "You will seek Me and find Me when you search for Me with all your heart" (Jer. 29:13).

It's always the right time to seek Him. Don't fear the future: God is already there, working on your behalf. God is for you.

Having an understanding there's more, opens you up to *all* God has for you.

There's always more than meets the eye. What you see is only part of the great big story God is writing.

5 Honestly Speaking?

My teacher asked me what my favorite animal was, and I said, "Fried chicken." She said that wasn't funny, but she couldn't have been right because everyone else laughed.

My parents told me to always tell the truth, so I did. Fried chicken is my favorite animal! I told my dad what happened, and he said my teacher was probably a member of PETA. He said they love animals very much. I do, too. Especially chicken, pork, and beef.

Anyway, my teacher sent me to the principal's office. I told him what happened, and he laughed, too. Then he told me not to do it again.

The next day in class, my teacher asked me what my favorite live animal was. I told her it was chicken. She asked me why, so I told her it was because you could make them into fried chicken. She sent me back to the principal's office. He laughed and said not to do it again.

I didn't understand. My parents taught me to be honest, but my teacher didn't like it when I was. The next day, my teacher asked me what famous person I admired most.

I told her, "Colonel Sanders." Guess where I was headed? (Story told by an anonymous person.)

Honesty will take you places you want to be...and sometimes places you may not want to be. But where you land will be better than if you're dishonest.

I simply don't want to be around people who don't understand the concept of loyalty and honesty.

Truth exists, but lies must be invented. The truth is more than enough. I worked for an organization in my thirties whose owner had a doctorate. In fact, it was made clear to every employee how important it was to address him as Dr. ——.

It wasn't long before I decided to investigate a little more about his degree. One day at work, I saw a framed document in a mostly neglected part of his office that decreed his PhD. It was for a discipline I was unfamiliar with, from a university I'd never heard of.

Upon further research, I discovered the "university" was a business that this particular owner had started several years earlier. He was "conferring" masters and doctorate degrees upon ministry and business associates...for a fee. In other words, he sold degrees and gave a "doctorate" to *himself!*

What a joke.

The next day, (I couldn't help myself) I began to ask other employees if they knew where he got his doctorate and for what discipline. They didn't, and it gave me a slight, wry joy to tell them "he had gotten it from himself."

I took it a step further. I declared to as many people as I could that I was also giving a doctorate to myself! From that day forward until now, most of the people who worked at that organization still refer to me as "Doc." One other humorous side story...

Later that year, I stopped a book right before it was sent to press with a foreword that identified me as Dr. John Mason. I guess some people thought I genuinely had a doctorate, or at least, that I had bought one.

If the words don't add up, it's usually because the truth wasn't included in the equation. I respect people who tell me the truth, no matter how hard it is.

If you tell the truth, it becomes a part of your past. If you tell a lie, it becomes a part of your future.

Just be honest with me…or stay away from me. I respect people with open intentions who tell me the truth every time. You and I must be honest with God, ourselves, and those we're closest to.

The truth is one thing for which there are no known substitutes. There is no acceptable substitute for honesty. There is no valid excuse for dishonesty.

Tell a lie once, and all your truths become questionable. Hope built on a lie is always the beginning of loss. There is no limit to the height you can attain by remaining on the level. Honesty is still the best policy.

6 You Make Mistakes, Mistakes Don't Make You.

—Maxwell Maltz

Sometimes I feel I'm an authority on failures and mistakes. I have so much experience…

Years ago I was invited to speak at a church I had never been to, for a pastor I had never met. I remember having an early-morning flight, so I was up before the break of dawn finishing my packing. I put everything in my suitcase and rushed off to the airport.

After thirty minutes in the air I began to replay my morning, checking off in my mind everything I had packed. Suit? Check. Shirts? Check. Shoes? Check.

Suddenly I wondered, *Did I bring my notes*? Yes. *My Bible*? Wait… I'm not sure. I immediately looked inside my carry-on bag. No Bible! It was nowhere to be found, no matter how many times I searched my bag.

I felt slightly panicked. Here I was, flying to a new church with a pastor I'd never met. I didn't want to walk off the plane, introduce myself, and then say, "Pastor, may I borrow your Bible?" I could only imagine him thinking, *Who have I entrusted my Sunday service to?*

I had to do something about this situation. I came up with what I thought was a good idea: I would get a Bible in the airport. Yes, I would find a bookstore and buy a Bible. But then I thought what you're probably thinking—*I've never seen a Bible for sale in the airport.* I began to get desperate.

I deplaned as fast as I could and made a beeline for the first store I could find selling books. "Do you sell Bibles?" I asked hopefully. "No," was the immediate response. I hurried to find another store. Again, I asked for a Bible. Again, the answer was no, but the clerk offered me some hope. She said, "I think the bookstore in the other terminal sells Bibles, so you should go there."

By then I should have been in baggage claim picking up my luggage, but I decided to run over to the other terminal in one last desperate attempt to secure a Bible.

Hurriedly, I moved from my current terminal to the other. I passed gate after gate before I saw a bookstore. I headed straight for the cashier, and, slightly out of breath, I asked, "Do you sell Bibles?"

"Yes, we do," she cheerfully replied. "Let me go get one for you." Relieved, I waited. Only a minute later, she appeared and handed me a small, white baptismal-type gift Bible. I'm thinking, *I didn't pack a white suit, white shirt, white tie, and white shoes. I can't preach from this little white Bible!* But I was desperate, so I went ahead and purchased it.

I quickly left the terminal and went down the escalator toward baggage claim. I was looking to my right and left as the moving steps went downward, hoping to see a "pastor-looking" person.

As I got to the bottom of the escalator, I saw a man alone looking all around. I knew I had found him.

I went straight up to him and introduced myself. He said, "Thank goodness it's you! Here's your bag—it was the only one left."

We walked to his car in the underground parking lot and left the airport. Five minutes into our ride he asked, "Would you like to go to the church before we go to the hotel? I'd like to show you our latest addition." Usually, I'd rather just head to my room. But suddenly I thought, *A church! They'll have Bibles!* I enthusiastically replied, "Yes!"

It wasn't long before we arrived at the church, and I made it a point to follow just a little behind him. We walked into the impressive main lobby. We continued toward the beautiful sanctuary. As we were about to enter, I spotted a box to my left. On it was a "lost and found" sign.

My heart began to beat a little faster; I was hoping my search was over with my dignity still intact. Following the pastor, I walked beside the box and looked inside. There it was, a beautiful Bible! In one smooth motion I reached in and "found" that Bible.

That whole weekend I preached with "my" new Bible. But in the back of my mind I wondered if someone out in the congregation was looking at me thinking, *That guy's got my Bible!*

Before I left the church, I discreetly returned the Bible to the lost and found, so whoever lost it could claim it. What a happy find that Bible was!

We all make mistakes. Some are funny, some affect us for a lifetime.

Everyone has struggles and regrets from the past. But you are not your mistakes.

The first step to overcoming mistakes is to admit them. You can't get past their hold without doing this. One of the most remarkable Scriptures promises us this, "If we confess our sins, He is faithful and just to forgive us our sins and to cleanse us from all unrighteousness" (1 John 1:9 NKJV). Wow! Thank you, God. Boy, have I needed this Bible verse in my life.

Our gracious God loves us so much. He forgives us, cleanses us, *and doesn't stop there*. He additionally gives us a right standing before God again. There is no way to fully express my gratitude to Him for this!

In Japan, broken objects are sometimes repaired with gold. The flaw is seen as a unique piece of the object's history, which adds to its beauty. Consider this when you feel broken by a bad action.

Don't let mistakes and disappointments of the past control and direct your future. They don't define you. You are free, when you give them to God.

7 You May Not Recognize This New Me; I'm Rearranging the Pieces.

Reaching my late forties, I began to realize I needed to use a bigger font for my sermon notes. I also started to read my Bible while I spoke with my right arm extended farther and farther out to see the words clearly. (Maybe you're nodding your head right now!)

One Sunday morning, I was ministering at a church in Southern California. The service was going well. I was sharing from the Word, with my Bible extended on my outstretched arm where I could see the words.

Right in the middle of my sermon, I couldn't help but notice a lady get up from her seat, turn down the center aisle, and walk out of the sanctuary. I thought about it for a second and then continued.

About ten minutes later, I saw that same lady return and walk down the center aisle, but instead of returning to her seat, she walked all the way to the pulpit where I was standing and handed me a box.

I stopped my message and opened the box. Inside was a brand-new large-print edition of the version of the Bible I was using. She had just purchased it in the church bookstore!

I've been using that Bible ever since.

Change is necessary. If you don't change, you'll be left behind. Like the printed words in that Bible, your life becomes more unclear when you don't adjust.

Sometimes you will discover what you need to change on your own. Other times, people will let you know. They will stop buying, stop listening, or just go away. No matter where or how the discovery comes, we all need to change to improve and grow.

Sadly, too many people associate staying the same with being spiritual.

Change is spiritual and painful. "But nothing is as painful as staying stuck somewhere you don't belong" (Mandy Hale).

"Change is inevitable. Growth is optional" (John C. Maxwell).

Christians should embrace change better than anyone else. We have the Holy Spirit to guide us! Many great Scriptures should give us comfort when we're facing change—passages that promise God will guide us with His eye, He will direct our steps, He'll be a light and lamp to our path and our feet.

It takes courage to let go of the familiar and embrace the new. If others don't embrace your change just tell them, "I'm currently under construction. Thank you for your patience."

The sad truth is most people are afraid of change.

Step out and make the change. People underestimate their capacity for change. There is never a perfect time to do a challenging thing. "Change is hard at first, messy in the middle, and gorgeous at the end" (Robin Sharma).

If you aren't changing, you're dying. If you change nothing, nothing will change.

Choose real change, not rearrangements like this lady made: "My husband wanted one of those big-screen TVs for his birthday. So, I just moved his chair closer to the one we have already" (Wendy Liebman).

When God wants you to grow, He makes you uncomfortable. Imagine if you just woke up one day next week and decided that you didn't want to feel the way you do anymore, or ever again? And you changed!

Rick Godwin says, "One reason people resist change is because they focus on what they have to give up, instead of what they have to gain."

"Your life does not get better by chance, it gets better by change" (Jim Rohn).

"Close some doors. Not because of pride, incapacity or arrogance, but simply because they no longer lead somewhere valuable" (Paulo Coelho).

It's amazing how drastically your life can change when you stop accepting the stuff you hate and embrace change.

8 Image Is Everything?

"Man looks at the outward appearance, but the Lord looks at the heart" (1 Sam. 16:7). Don't get duped into thinking that your life is less than a seemingly ideal person's life. Everyone has faults.

Comparison is never proof. There's a crack in everything... that's how the light and bugs get in.

Back before cell phones were so commonplace, it was critical to have a watch when you traveled. There was no other way to tell time except for public clocks.

I had a certain watch I liked to wear on the road. It was nice and comfortable. It kept accurate time, too.

I had just returned from consulting a church in Sweden when I received a small package from the pastor's associate and his administrator—a beautiful Rolex Presidential watch! Yes, the one with a solid gold face and diamonds all around it. Unfortunately, this one was a fake, but boy, did it look real. I'm sure the guys sent it to me as a half gift, half joke.

As I packed for a trip to consult a church in Missouri, I was arranging all my usual items when I realized I couldn't locate my favorite watch. The nice, comfortable one.

As the time drew near for me to leave for the airport, I knew I had a decision to make. No watch, or wear the fake Rolex watch. I reluctantly picked the "Rolex."

After I landed and rode in the car toward our meeting place, I did my best to keep the watch as out of sight as I could. It stood out, and I wasn't sure how the pastor might respond to someone in my position wearing it.

Finally our meeting began—just the pastor and me in a conference room sitting across the table from each other.

After a couple of minutes of small talk, I noticed the pastor was wearing a beautiful Rolex himself. I began to feel more comfortable. Until he looked at me, then my watch, and asked, "Is that a fake?"

"Yes," I replied. "Mine is too," he said. We both laughed and still chuckle about it now, thirty years later. The only difference now is that he has a *real* Rolex and I'm using my cell phone to tell time.

When image becomes more important than truth (reality), there is a reason—and a problem.

For many people, the saying is "just as I'm not," not "just as I am."

Speaking of "just as I am," famous author and evangelist, Billy Graham, wrote a book that was essentially his life story several years ago. That book was entitled, *Just as I Am*. This was a great title for his book because it was based on the song that he played at nearly every one of his crusades.

At the exact same time that Billy Graham's book was published, another book was released, ironically or coincidentally, with the exact same title, *Just as I Am*. That book was a homosexual novel.

Now I know this example could leave you feeling perplexed, but it reflects the fact that titles are not copyrightable. In fact, I went to a local Barnes & Noble and saw Billy Graham's book prominently displayed, and wouldn't you know it, only one table over I saw the exact same title… that novel, *Just as I Am*.

Both books appeared the same on the outside, but what a difference on the inside!

"The Christian life is not about managing your reputation so you look like a Christian. It's about handing Jesus your heart, your will, your emotions, your ambitions (everything really), and asking Him to live His amazing life through you. The first is playacting; the other is genuine Jesus-loving faith" (Mary DeMuth).

We should be the same person privately, publicly, and personally.

"Most people are other people. Their thoughts are someone else's opinions, their lives a mimicry, their passions a quotation" (Oscar Wilde).

Be inspired, but don't copy. Nothing is more inspiring than a confident person who doesn't pretend to be something they're not.

If you're someone else when you're with others, you'll have to remember who you were the next time you're with them.

Is faking it a way of life for you?

For some people, it's not merely "fake it until you make it." It's fake it until you fake it until you fake it until you fake it. Be careful who you pretend to be. You might forget who you are.

9 Thoroughly Enjoy Minding Your Own Business.

Alaska was one state I'd never been to until I received an invitation to speak at a conference hosted by a thriving church in Anchorage. It was a two-day conference, and I was honored to be the guest speaker.

The conference was going very well, with overflow crowds on both sides of the aisle of the church. I was well into my message on the first evening when right in the middle of my talk a man shouted out, "Does that apply to your wife too?" Slightly stunned at the interruption, I replied, "Of course." I continued speaking, all the while wondering what that was about. To this day, I don't remember what I said that prompted that response.

As I was ending my message, I noticed all the ushers positioning themselves nearby along the walls near the front of the church. As I closed the service and walked off the platform, I saw the man who had shouted out during the service walking briskly toward me. Simultaneously, all the ushers began to converge in my direction to position themselves between the man and me. I began to wonder if this guy was dangerous.

Before the man could get to me, I was completely encircled by the ushers. Still, he was able to call out to me, "I'm sorry for saying that while you were speaking." I told him, "No problem," and he left without further incident.

After the service, I went to dinner with the pastor and his wife. I couldn't help but ask, "What was the deal with the guy who spoke out tonight?"

The pastor looked at me with an expression of "you won't believe this." He said, "The man you heard in the service has been in our church several years. He is a former police officer. His beat was the airport.

"A year or so ago, he was working and got into a dispute with a teenager out near the airport. The altercation escalated, and the youth fled. He pursued the young man, got into a scuffle with him, shot, and killed him."

Apparently, it was unclear whether the killing was justified, and the police officer was currently under investigation.

"Furthermore, I learned the whole incident had affected his personality and his family. His wife left him and took off with another man. She was here tonight, with the other man, right across the aisle from him. That was the reason for his comment, 'Does that apply to your wife too?'

"There also was a shooting a year ago of a minister in a service nearby, so everyone was aware of that too."

Everyone except me, I thought.

What did I learn from this? Sometimes less is more. Sometimes it's better not to know everything. And…it's always better to stay out of other people's troubles.

Can you imagine my state of mind if I had known all this before and while I spoke? I'm sure I would have been distracted and not as focused as I should be. Although I somehow put my words into this man's situation between his wife and him, I certainly didn't do it on purpose. I know better!

"Like one who grabs a stray dog by the ears is someone who rushes into a quarrel not their own" (Prov. 26:17 NIV). Don't trouble trouble, until trouble troubles you.

"How do I have productive days with minimum drama? Simple; I mind my own business" (Dr. Steve Maraboli). Nothing will bring you greater peace than staying out of other people's business.

The more you get involved, the more you'll be sucked in. Your best ideas and energies will be absorbed in the sponge of someone else's troubles.

Instead, turn away toward your own destiny.

Worry about your own sins; you will not be asked about someone else's. How will getting involved in other people's issues and problems help you pay your bills?

"Mind your own biscuits and life will be gravy" (Kacey Musgraves).

10 Weakness Is the Sweet Spot Where God Can Do the Most Work.

My wife and I decided to have a cup of coffee at the local IHOP restaurant. After being seated in a booth near the front, we were quickly greeted by a very friendly, happy, smiling waitress. It didn't take long to notice our cheerful helper had only one tooth—it was on top and smack-dab in the middle. I thought, *Isn't that interesting! Here is a woman with one tooth, yet she works in a job that requires a lot of people contact* (up close). *She's smiling, doing a good job.*

Then my eyes were drawn to a button she was wearing. It said, "A smile is a gift you can give every day." What a profound scene this was! So much so that I complimented her on her button and sincerely told her she had a nice smile. I wondered if anyone had told her that lately—or ever.

Hunt for the good points in people. Remember, they must do the same in your case. Then, do something to help them.

When she returned to our table to refill our coffee, she told me her father had done the calligraphy on the button. She said, "He had his fingers cut off in an industrial accident, and *then* decided to pick up calligraphy after that!" In fact, she told us that his writing was now better than before the accident.

I immediately thought, *I guess only a lady who was raised by a dad with no fingers who does calligraphy can choose to smile even though she has only one tooth.*

Thomas Edison was afraid of the dark. But Edison took what he had and made the most of it. His invention of electricity and the consequent lightbulb took on his fears directly. We should too.

Strength doesn't come from what you can do. It comes from overcoming the things you once thought you couldn't.

Don't let the weakness in you affect the greatness in you.

You might have more than one tooth (I certainly hope so). But I promise, you have other "deficiencies" that are a part of the perfectly imperfect way God made you.

"My grace is sufficient for you, for power is perfected in weakness. Most gladly, therefore, I will rather boast about my weaknesses, so that the power of Christ may dwell in me. Therefore I am well content with weaknesses, with insults, with distresses, with persecutions, with difficulties, for Christ's sake; for when I am weak, then I am strong" (2 Cor. 12:9-10).

Give God your weakness, and He will give you His strength. Sometimes we're tested, not to expose our weaknesses, but to discover our strengths.

Never underestimate your strength, never overestimate your weakness. Don't let them hold you back. Turn them from liabilities into assets. Successful people take what they have, *no matter what it looks like*, are thankful, and then go and make the most of it.

11 Do One Thing Every Day that Scares You.

— Eleanor Roosevelt

I had just begun to go out and minister in churches, and this was my third official opportunity.

I found myself in a storefront church in Tampa, Florida, speaking for a bright young pastor. I was naive, inexperienced, excited, and willing to do anything for God. Life was wide open, and I was running full speed ahead.

I remember speaking to about one hundred people that Sunday night, sharing from my heart as well as I could. As I finished my message, I felt I should offer the people an opportunity for prayer at the altar. Whatever their need, I was going to pray with them about it.

I laid hands on and prayed for the ten or so people who came forward. As I neared the last person, I came to a young man who asked me to pray for his tongue. I immediately told him to stick out his tongue. I grabbed his tongue with my right hand and began to pray earnestly for it. I know I was probably freaking this kid out, but I went ahead.

After the service, I was outside talking with several church members when the young man with the "tongue issue" came over to me. He said, "Thank you for praying for me and my tongue. I had a stuttering problem, but God has healed my words tonight."

Wow! God is good. I'll never forget what He did for that boy. I wonder if I would grab a tongue now that I'm more "experienced" and "wiser"? I hope I would if that's what it takes.

Now, weird doesn't equal spiritual. But that said, God may ask you to do something way outside your comfort zone. In fact, I promise you He will. Jesus once used spit to heal. He may ask you to get your hands dirty (or wet in my case) to do His will.

"The scariest paths often lead you to the most exciting places" (Lori Deschene). It's OK to be "spiritually uncomfortable." Because when you are, you're about to do something really, really, brave.

I've tried to follow this saying my whole life: *"Be instant to obey, taking action without delay."* I know the longer I think, ponder, or even pray about something, the less likely I am to do it.

The longer it takes to act on God's direction, the more unclear it will become.

Step out of your comfort zone. You're not alone. If He directed you, He won't leave you hanging.

There might be a tongue out there waiting for you!

12 Every Destiny Requires a First Step.

The phone rang in my office. I answered, and on the other end was a voice saying, "John, I've heard about the consulting work you do with churches. I'd like to fly you up to Minneapolis to interview you about using your services and have you give your opinion about an issue that's before our board right now."

I responded saying, "Of course, I'd be honored to come and meet with you and your board. And hopefully be able to consult your church in the future."

I wanted to say more, but the pastor interrupted me by asking, "Do you preach too?" I hesitated. I hadn't preached yet, but the Lord had been leading me to start preaching, so I said, "Yes, I preach."

"Fine. I want you to come like we described, and also preach in the Sunday morning and Sunday evening services. We're a small inner-city church so, I can only give you one hundred dollars." I said yes. I was now committed, surprised, and a little nervous.

I flew into the Twin Cities, and the pastor met me at the airport... in a full-length mink coat! We went from baggage claim straight to his car, a new BMW 7 Series. I was thinking, *Something is wrong with this picture.*

Briefly, he took me to the church before heading to the hotel. The church was downtown and looked to have a seating capacity of a couple of hundred. I went to my room to prepare for the next day's meetings and messages.

This was my very first time to preach in a church, so I awoke with an excitement I had not had before. I was looking forward to sharing with his congregation.

The service began like most services—people singing, congregants sharing announcements, and prayer requests. Then it was time for the sermon.

The pastor eloquently introduced me. I rose from my seat on the front row. Bounded up the steps toward the pulpit. Missed the last step…and fell flat on my face!

What a way to launch my preaching career! I gathered myself, walked behind the pulpit, and said, "Now that I have your attention…" and began my message.

The people responded well, and I gave it my all. As I was closing, I sensed in my heart that I should give an invitation for prayer. I invited people to come to the altar for prayer for any need they had.

I prayed for each person who came. As I was almost finished, I saw a young man near the end of the line. His head was bowed, and he turned to me and asked for prayer. As soon as I began to pray for him, I felt strongly that I should pray for his family—more specifically, for his relationship with his father. So, I did, out loud.

I had no idea at the time, but I learned shortly afterward that his father was the pastor who had invited me to speak! He was rather upset with my public prayer for his son, and again I felt like, *What a start!*

He told me in his office I was now not going to speak at the evening service. But things got worse when the pastor shared with me what he wanted me to agree with him about and present to the board.

He wanted me to present an idea (without getting into any detail) I knew was certainly wrong. It was now obvious he had brought me up there to give his idea credibility. I refused to do it.

I don't remember if he gave me the hundred dollars. He probably did. But what is most interesting is what happened next.

Three weeks later he left the church and his wife. He left her alone to pastor the church, which she faithfully did for many years.

About fifteen years after this experience, I was speaking at a pastors' conference. At the break, a nice young man came up to me and asked me if I recognized him or knew who he was. I told him, "I'm sorry, I don't."

He said, "You prayed for me at my father's church years ago. God used you that day. My situation was bad, but I knew I couldn't tell anyone. My mom is doing well, and I'm now married, volunteering at the church, and I have a young child. We are all serving the Lord!"

Don't judge how you *start* on God's path for you as an indication of how well or not so well it will go. You may fall flat on your face, or you may get out of the gate like Secretariat. Either way, the only way to go forward is to be submitted to His will, committed to serving others, and to always tell the truth. *Just begin*, and you will find yourself halfway there.

The Bible reminds us not to despise the day of small beginnings. Or as Pat Robertson once shared, "Despise not the day of small beginnings because you can make all your mistakes anonymously."

"The scariest moment is always just before you start. If you don't go after what you want, you'll never have it. If you don't ask, the answer will always be no. If you don't step forward, you will always be in the same place" (Anonymous).

"Sometimes the smallest step in the right direction ends up being the biggest step of your life. Tiptoe if you must, but take the step" (Naeem Callaway).

Right where you are is the best place to start. Big things often have small beginnings. You'll discover the importance of going forward once you've taken the first step.

Faith is taking the first step even when you can't see the whole staircase.

My beginning mistakes are now not so anonymous because of this book. But I wouldn't trade those experiences and lessons for anything. God looks at your heart, not your eloquence...or your ability to climb the steps without falling.

13 Go to Sleep with a Dream and Wake Up with a Purpose.

I had the opportunity to work for the largest Christian publisher in America. In my role as vice president and publisher, I oversaw all publishing and book acquisitions from authors in the nondenominational Christian world. In this role, I interacted with many leading ministers and pastors. Of course, quite a few other people wanted to contact me to see if we would publish their books as well.

I'll never forget one such encounter. I received a call from a man I had heard about but didn't know personally. As soon as our conversation began, he told me he had five great book ideas, and that they would easily sell a million copies each. (Telling this to a person like me is a bad idea.) I listened to what each book was about. They were decent ideas, but nothing particularly unique. And there was no way they would sell as he thought.

I think he could sense my hesitancy as he continued to up the ante with his sales pitch for his books. He said, "I'm blessed, and if you do a book with me, you'll be blessed." I had heard this line before. He continued to tell me that I would make millions because of my association with him.

So, I decided to ask him a question. I said, "*Why* are you writing these books?" hoping he would share a good motive behind them.

He instead told me, "Well, I want to be rich!" I remember thinking, *I thought you were already wealthy.*

I told him I needed a couple of days and that I would get back to him. I was 99 percent sure I knew what my decision would be. I called him back a couple of days later and told him we were going to pass on his books, that they weren't a fit for us at that time. He was angry about my decision. He told me I was "missing God" and urged me to reconsider. I said my answer was final, but I wished him the best.

Only a couple of years later that man was all over the national news. A major marital fight in public, a messy divorce, and lots of other junk exposed.

Hearing this hammered home to me how important purpose is. The *why* behind your action and ideas matters a great deal.

Jacob Nordby said, "You know how every once in a while you do something and the little voice inside says, 'There. That's it. That's why you're here.' ...and you get a warm glow in your heart because you know it's true? Do more of that."

If you can't figure out your purpose, figure out your passion. Your passion will lead you right into your purpose.

"Pay attention to the things you are naturally drawn to. They are often connected to your path, passion, and purpose in life. Have the courage to follow them" (Ruben Chavez).

You can't pour from an empty cup. Fill up on your purpose, and you'll be able to share it with others. William Shakespeare said, "The meaning of life is to find your gift. The purpose of life is to give it away."

How amazing is it that the same God who created mountains, oceans, and galaxies, looked at you and thought the world needed one of you too!

Harold Whitman said, "Don't ask yourself what the world needs; ask yourself what makes you come alive. And then go and do that. Because what the world needs are people who have come alive."

"Your life has a purpose. Your story is important. Your dreams count. Your voice matters. You were born to make an impact" (Unknown).

"Be fearless in the pursuit of what sets your soul on fire" (Unknown). Our prayer should be, "Use me, God. Show me how to take who I am, who I want to be, and what I can do, and use it for a purpose greater than myself" (Martin Luther King Jr).

14 Stop Yourself from Stopping Yourself.

I had finished my day at the office and was getting up from my desk to walk out of the building when I noticed I had a bump on my knee. This bump was so big, it made my pants stick out on the right side of my knee.

I didn't bang my knee on anything! I thought. *What could it be?* I began to replay my day over and over again, convincing myself I had not bumped my knee on anything.

You know, you should not build a case against yourself. Don't put water in your own boat; the storm will put enough in on its own. And did you know that the great evangelist Dwight L. Moody said, "I've never met a man who gave me as much trouble as myself"?

I knew I hadn't bumped my knee on anything, and as I thought about it, a second thought came to me… *I've had bumps before, but this feels different! It doesn't feel like a bump. It feels like a lump!*

After five minutes of thinking like this, I remember suddenly picturing myself playing golf with only one leg!

You see, through fear and worry, I'd gone from a *bump* to a *lump* to a *stump*! In only five minutes.

By then I was driving home, and suddenly I realized what I was doing. I said out loud, "John, you're so stupid! I thank you, God, that by Jesus' stripes I was healed. Your Word says believers can lay their hands on the sick and they recover!"

I laid my hand on my knee, said a prayer, and by the time I got home that bump was completely gone.

There is nothing in this world that can trouble you as much as your own thoughts. No one has the right to make you feel badly, not even you.

"My enemy said to me, 'Love your enemy.' And I obeyed him and loved myself" (Khalil Gibran). Look in the mirror—that's your competition. Your worst enemy can't harm you as much as your own unfiltered thoughts.

I keep my friends close and my enemies closer—that's easy for most of us to do when we're our own worst enemy.

> Don't believe the things you think,
> in the middle of the night.
> You're your own worst enemy,
> and you can't win that fight. (Unknown)

When bumps come your way, here's how to win: you can keep "casting down imaginations, and every high thing that is exalted against the knowledge of God, and bringing every thought into captivity to the obedience of Christ" (2 Cor. 10:5 ASV).

Don't believe everything you think. "There are plenty of difficult obstacles in your path. Don't allow yourself to become one of them" Ralph Marston).

15 Think This: "I Will Never Apologize for Being Me. You Should Apologize for Asking Me to Be Anything Else."

—Unknown

Early in my career, I was a consultant to a new church and school. As was the case with private Christian schools, they had an honor code that students and staff were expected to sign and adhere to. I soon discovered that the entire honor code was entirely built around how the pastor looked, dressed, talked, and believed. Imagine a forty-plus-year-old person as the standard for kids ages five through eighteen.

It didn't take me long to find out that the more you were like the leader, the more you were celebrated. The less you were like him, the more you were criticized. People there found themselves using their leader's phrases to express themselves, instead of their own.

Of course, those who don't fit into a box like this are always labeled rebellious and disobedient.

When you work with people who have found the solution to what they believe is the perfect Christian model, you find out they never know what to do with individuals who don't fit.

There is no single, right Christian model other than Jesus. "I don't believe we were put here with all of our differences to conform to a uniform state of mind" (Sonya Teclai).

Romans 12:2 says, "Don't copy the behavior and customs of this world, but be a new and different person with a fresh newness in all you do and think. Then you will learn from your own experience how his ways will really satisfy you" (TLB).

We aren't called to be like other Christians; we are called to be like Christ.

God creates completely unique individuals, whereas too many leaders are inventing a single mold to which all must conform. And it usually looks, talks, and acts like them. It's laughable.

Steve Jobs said, "When you grow up, you tend to get told that the world is the way it is and your life is just to live your life inside the world. 'Try not to bash into the walls too much.' 'Try to have a nice family.' 'Have fun.' 'Save a little money.' That's a very limited life. Life can be much broader once you discover one simple fact: Everything around you that you call life was made up by people who were no smarter than you. And you can change it, you can influence it.... Once you learn that, you will never be the same again."

People may hate you for being yourself, but deep down they wish they had the courage to do the same.

"Be daring, be different, be impractical, be anything that will assert integrity of purpose and imaginative vision against the 'play—it—safers,' the creatures of the commonplace, the slaves of the ordinary" (Sir Cecil Beaton).

God loves variety! There are more than twenty thousand known species of ferns growing around the world. They are universally recognized as one of the hardiest plants. I know it doesn't make sense to us that God made that many different kinds, but they show us how much He loves diversity.

In a controlling environment, conformity is celebrated. You can fall into the trap of judging how you're doing spiritually by how much you act, sound, and look like the leader. Imagine if the body of Christ all looked like a foot, an ear, or an arm?

People say, "Be yourself." But when you are, they say, "Not like that." Don't waste time trying to be someone else. Everybody likes conformity...except for the person who must conform.

Some people will only love you if you fit into their box. Don't be afraid to disappoint them. Life isn't about finding yourself; it is about discovering who God created you to be.

16 There Is Nothing Wrong with Change If It's in the Right Direction.

Awhile back it became very popular for families to hang a yellow diamond-shaped "Baby On Board" sign in the rear windshields of their cars. You could find these signs in the back windows of minivans and SUVs all over America.

I purchased one of those yellow signs, but mine said "Stunt Driver." I must admit, that sign made me laugh, and friends of mine who saw it got a chuckle out of it, too. But all the laughter stopped one day on my way home from work.

I left my office right at rush hour and was trying to merge onto a busy highway to head home at the end of the day. The street I was merging onto was a one-way street from left to right. So of course, I was looking to my left, trying to judge when would be the best time to pull out into traffic and then merge onto the highway.

I had done this hundreds of occasions on my way home from work, usually at the same time with the same busyness. I would ease my way onto the highway safely and then head on home for dinner.

This day seemed like any other; I was patiently waiting my turn to pull out. I saw an opening, and I began to merge onto the highway when I heard a big thump on the right side of my car!

I immediately pulled to the side of the road, stopped, and looked into my rearview mirror...only to see a person sprawled out in the middle of the road with a bicycle beside him.

I cautiously pulled off onto a side street. The first thing that came to mind wasn't how I was going to help this person, but rather, *Oh no! I've just collided into somebody, and I have a stunt driver sign in my back window!*

I scrambled to the backseat of my car, reached up, and tore the sign from my window. I didn't want anyone, especially a police officer, to know that I thought I was a "stunt driver." I got out of my car, and by the time I got to the person in the street, there was already a lady there praying over him.

He had been biking the wrong way on a one-way street. As I pulled out, he ran into my car bumper, flew over the top of my car, and landed on the road, instantly breaking his leg. He was obviously in a lot of pain, and I felt very sorry for him.

The police arrived in a matter of minutes. I'll never forget the police officer coming over to me, listening to me talk about what happened, and then saying, "I guess he learned his lesson. Going down a one-way street the wrong way is a formula for disaster."

Speeding along the wrong way may work for a while, even a long while. But eventually, something bad will probably happen. What benefit is running, if you're on the wrong road? "It is better to go slow in the right direction than to go fast in the wrong direction" (Simon Sinek).

No matter how long you've traveled in the wrong direction, you can still turn around.

"It is better to walk alone, than with a crowd going in the wrong direction" (Herman Siu). The one who follows the crowd will usually get no further than the crowd. Stop chasing the wrong path.

Many times, the action you take at the right time has no immediate relationship to the end result—but it gets you to the right place at the right time going the right direction.

Be careful about rushing God's timing and changing His direction. You never know who or what He is protecting you or saving you from.

Nothing good happens to us when we choose to go the wrong way, especially when the right path is in the opposite direction. In the case of this man, I wonder if he had done this many times, with no issues. But one day, he encountered an obstacle that stopped him (my car). I guarantee that when he could get back on his bike, he never went down that one-way street the wrong way again.

PART II

Have Hope, Give Hope

17 You Didn't Come This Far Only to Come This Far.

It's 1943, and World War II is raging.

A young boy is standing on a downtown Jackson, Mississippi, street corner every day selling newspapers early in the morning and late into the evening. At the same time, he's selling war stamps to support the war effort.

Born in the charity hospital, he is being raised in the poorest part of town, and most of his young friends are now in jail. He has no brothers, no sisters, no aunts, no uncles. Since his father passed away, he has been the sole provider for his illiterate mother and himself since age ten.

There's a contest across the country to see who can sell the most war stamps.

This boy, the most unlikely of success stories, has sold twelve million dollars' worth of war stamps. The second-place finisher? Four million dollars.

As a result, he wins a trip to meet the president of the United States, and with a borrowed suit two sizes too big, heads off to Washington DC for a journey of a lifetime.

Later, this young man serves his community as a firefighter for nine years and one day rescues a young girl no one else can save. He graduates from Hines Junior College in Mississippi, then marries a pretty brunette from Indiana, and soon after graduates from the Indiana University School of Business.

After serving his country in the army, he runs a successful branch office for his employer, earning more than thirty consecutive years of profit. All the while, he never loses the balance of loving his wife, loving his kids, and loving his God.

A real success in my eyes. Ultimate success.

He was the best man at my wedding. He's easily the hardest-working man I have ever worked with. And when you consider where he started, the obstacles he overcame, and how he ended up, he's the most successful man I know.

Today I think of him as I write this book. You see, that boy was my dad, Chester Mason. Against all the odds and despite all the obstacles, he made it.

My dad never made a big deal about what he had to overcome. He just did it because he didn't want to stay where he was and he wanted a better life for himself and his family.

So sometimes when I find myself doubting how far I can go, I just remember how far my dad came in life. I saw everything he faced, all the battles he won, and all the fears he overcame. All the best stories have one thing in common: you must go against the odds to reach your dreams.

When you focus on problems, you'll have more problems. When you focus on possibilities, you'll have more opportunities. When someone tells you "it can't be done," it's more of a reflection of their limitations, not yours.

Overcoming obstacles not only impacts your life, but all those connected to you now and in the future. If you are unsure about pressing on, remember there are others depending on you.

The secret to ultimate success is to take what you have, be thankful for it, then go out and make the very most of it. No obstacle leaves you the way it found you. God knows that obstacles along your journey are there to prepare you for the blessings that await you at the finish line.

When I consider my dad's life, I agree with Booker T. Washington when he said, "I have learned that success is to be measured not so much by the position that one has reached in life, as by the obstacles which he has overcome while trying to succeed."

18 Miracles Come in Moments.

I was invited to speak at an early-morning devotional, and they asked me to talk for twenty minutes. I remember working on my notes for the talk on a legal pad with green pages. I don't think I've ever used that color paper before, or since.

My notes for this talk included thirty-five points. I had twenty minutes. Little did I know then that covering a lot of ideas in a short amount of time would be the basis for writing my best-selling books.

The night before, I went to bed earlier than normal. When I woke up, I wasn't asking my usual questions—what time is it, what should I wear, where did I leave my keys? No, instead, my *very first thought* was, *An Enemy Called Average.* Yes, not only was God giving me, I believe, a title for my talk, but also a great title for the book I was writing.

I remember writing that phrase at the top of my notes, and then proclaiming to my audience, "Today, I want to share with you about An Enemy Called Average." After my speech, I had several people come up to me and say, "That's a great book title." I told them, "I know, it's mine—don't take it!" with a smile.

I didn't have a clue how much that phrase and that book would impact my life and hundreds of thousands of others around the world.

I kept my original notes on that green legal paper. Recently, my daughter, Michelle, surprised me by beautifully framing them. When I opened her gift, it brought tears to my eyes as I was reminded how God, in His love for people, gave me that phrase. It was God's miraculous deposit into my heart that morning.

I think we should live, to paraphrase Oral Roberts, "expecting a miracle." Not in a strange sense where we overspiritualize everything but aware that the Maker of the Universe is our Father. And He is well able to *do anything, at anytime, anywhere.*

I am a realist: I expect miracles at any time. I try my best to have a holy suspicion that God is up to something good every day.

Sometimes, God just drops something in your lap for you to share. He does that because He loves people. He's trusting you and me to do something with it to bless others.

Miracles happen every day, so never stop believing. God can change things very quickly in your life. Open your heart and invite God into every circumstance, because when God enters the scene, miracles happen.

The question is not, "Does God speak?" The question is, "Are we listening?"

Writing the book started as a dream, an impossible kind of hope. Sometimes I wonder if I ever would have finished that book without that divinely-given title.

The moment you're ready to quit is usually the moment right before a miracle happens.

You and I have two choices. Live your life as though nothing is a miracle, or that everything is a miracle. I choose the latter. How about you?

19 Keep Going. Everything You Need Will Come to You at the Right Time.

I decided to be a business administration major during the beginning of my freshman year of college. I concluded that this degree would offer me the best post-college job opportunities, and I admired my dad who was a businessman.

I enrolled in the basic freshman-level business courses—principles of management, economics, and accounting 101.

I'll never forget my first day in accounting class. Since I hadn't decided to study business until a few weeks earlier, I quickly discovered that most of my classmates had taken bookkeeping in high school. This gave them a basic understanding of accounting, so on that very first day, I felt like I was already two months behind.

Our instructor was a very popular teacher. He was also known as demanding, and gave tests no one could complete on time.

Moreover, I didn't like the subject. It almost felt like a foreign language to me. If you know anything about accounting, most of it flies in the face of logic. Many things you think would be debits are posted as credits and credits posted as debits. Confusing, to say the least.

The final kicker was that accounting was required to graduate with my chosen degree. Two years of it!

I was determined to give it my best, and candidly, my loftiest goal was to get a C. That was the minimum required. It was tough for me.

Each of our homework assignments were to be completed on green ledger paper with a #2 pencil. I remember taking hours to do each task, and there were a lot of them!

After spending hours on one assignment, I just couldn't get it to balance. And balancing a ledger is the fundamental goal for all accounting. As much as I tried, I was off by eleven cents!

What happened next was about to make me somewhat of a legend in the business school.

I did what made sense to me. I taped a dime and a penny to my homework and gave it to my instructor with this note: "Here is the $0.11 I can't find in this assignment. I hope this takes care of it. I plan to go into marketing and make enough money after I graduate to have someone else do my accounting for me. Sincerely, John Mason."

Here's the point.

One of the biggest understatements in the Bible is "My thoughts are not your thoughts, nor are your ways My ways," declares the Lord. "For as the heavens are higher than the earth, so are My ways higher than your ways and My thoughts than your thoughts" (Isa. 55:8-9).

We can't even imagine *all* that He can do. He may not always give you want you want, how you want it, and where you want it. We can try and treat Him like an on-demand God, but that isn't how He moves in our lives. Trust me, He has a better plan.

Mankind says show me and I'll trust you. God says trust Me and I'll show you. His solutions are vast. His way is infinitely higher than our ways and it is perfect.

Sometimes He will deliver you directly from your situation, but sometimes He'll find a way around or through it for you.

I'm not saying God directed me to tape that money on my homework (that would be a stretch), but I do know there are many ways God can get you where He wants you to be. Don't limit Him. Be open to every idea and path He provides for you.

20 The Best Thing to Appreciate in Life Is Each Other.

Not long after The Affordable Care Act (also known as Obamacare) became law, we received a most unusual call in our office. The caller identified herself as a top leader within the United States Department of Human Services. She said her team was responsible for the implementation of Obamacare and that they desperately needed encouragement.

If anyone needed a boost, these folks did.

It seems she had read my book, *An Enemy Called Average*, and was now inviting me to speak to the entire leadership team of about fifty top government staffers. The group included many significant civil servants from several branches of the government. She also let me know that these leaders were not political appointees but long-term employees. Some agreed with Obamacare, and some didn't. Nevertheless, it was their job to make it work, as they had for President George Bush's prescription drug program a few years earlier.

At first my daughter, Michelle, who took the call, thought it was a prank. The rollout of this program had been a national joke, with troubles in its website, availability, and information—the list went on and on.

I talked at length with the caller about their situation and how they had worked day and night, weekends and holidays, trying to right this enormous government ship. Most had taken very few days off since this had become law. These employees were senior executives, with most having worked for the federal government for twenty or thirty years, or more.

She also informed me about guidelines for speakers—no religious comments and no political views. That roomful of employees would be as diverse as I could imagine, of every religious, political, ethnic, sexual, and philosophical persuasion imaginable.

I was out of my comfort zone, *right where I'm supposed to be*, I thought. God was stretching me, and I knew that when He does that, I never return to my original shape. I was excited!

I prepared, working on what I was going to say—and what I wasn't. I felt confident I could serve them well with my talk. And they were allowing questions after I finished, something I enjoy doing!

The day of my talk, security was tight. A senior military leader picked me up, and when we arrived at our destination, I went through several checkpoints. I remember as I sat in the car and journeyed toward the meeting, I began to have a thought I couldn't shake: these individuals were faithfully doing their jobs under enormous pressure, and they were hammered with criticism they had done nothing to deserve. I knew what I had to tell them before I began my talk.

I'm sure you've done this. You see a military person or a police officer dressed in uniform, maybe on a plane, in a store, or at a public event. You go up to them and tell them, "Thank you for your service." It made you feel good, and hopefully, it made them feel good also.

I began to feel this way toward these civil servants for the effort they were displaying. Not only for their work amid the disastrous lack of foresight in this law, but also for the decades of service they had given to our country...and to me.

After being introduced, I stood before the group. The look in most of their eyes told me they'd rather be somewhere else. *Anywhere else*. It was not a friendly Sunday-morning crowd. I told them I had something to say to them from my heart before I began. I looked them straight in the eye and said, "Thank you for *your* service!"

You could not believe the immediate change in the countenance of everyone I could see. A simple word of encouragement, a thank-you given. It was so powerful.

The talk went well. The questions afterward went quickly from business to personal, and people opened their lives to me. I shared from my life how I depend on God to help me.

As we ate a catered lunch together after the talk and questions, many people came up to me and said, "I've been working for the government for twenty-plus years, and *no one* has ever thanked me for my service. You did. You will never know how much that meant to me."

I had no idea those simple words, "I appreciate your service" would touch people so deeply.

Never underestimate the power of a simple thank-you and random compliments. How long has it been since you've thanked those closest to you or those you interact with every day? Just imagine for a moment what your life would look like if you did.

Never waste an opportunity to tell someone that you love and appreciate them, because you never know, tomorrow could be too late. A good way to appreciate someone is to imagine your life without them.

Reach out and appreciate those closest to you every day. Because what we do every day matters!

I believe our genuine self is a grateful self. One that is appreciative of others and shares that gratitude. A simple thank-you or an encouraging word can be so powerful. You don't have to agree on everything, just be there with a "word in due season." You'll be surprised at the good it might do.

21 "Trust Me," God Whispers.

Linda and I were struggling financially like any young married couple who had a child or two. I needed a better job with better pay. We began to agree, in prayer, specifically for an opportunity doing certain things for a good salary. We asked God for what we thought we'd need to make financially.

Within a week or two, I received a phone call out of the blue about an opportunity to be a church administrator at a rapidly growing church in Southern California.

Incredibly, the job description was what we prayed for. In fact, it was all I desired, plus freedom to continue to consult. The salary was excellent and what we hoped for. It seemed, at the time, to be the precise answer to prayer that we petitioned God for.

I remember my first conversation with the senior pastor about the job. He told me I had come highly recommended from another church that was a consulting client of mine, and he was very excited to have Linda, both our children, and me fly out to California to interview for the position.

Within a matter of weeks, we arrived in California for this job opportunity. The day after we arrived, we went to Disneyland with the pastor and his wife. Candidly, they rolled out the red carpet for me, and it seemed like everything was perfect.

Except that Linda and I both felt something wasn't quite right. But how could that be? This appeared to be the perfect answer to prayer. It was exactly what we had asked for—and more!

Upon returning to Tulsa a week later, the pastor called me and excitedly offered me the job. That unsettled feeling inside of me was still there, so I told him I needed to think about it. He seemed to be quite surprised and slightly irritated at my response. I said I would get back with him within a day or two.

The opportunity at the church was good. It was the most rapidly growing church in his denomination, and he was a tremendous speaker. They were having multiple services and standing-room-only crowds. It was a beautiful part of the country; everything looked *right*. But, it was *wrong*.

I called the pastor back and told him that I was going to decline the offer. I was a little taken aback at his angry retort. He said that I was missing God's will and that it was *right* for me to take this job. He pressed and asked if I would reconsider. I sincerely told him I would give it another consideration and get back to him.

Over the next couple of days, I talked with Linda and prayed about this opportunity that looked so perfect on the surface. But the more we talked and prayed, the more we were sure that it definitely wasn't right. *Even though it was exactly what we prayed for.*

I called the pastor back, and I told him I was not taking the job and my decision was final. He flatly told me I was missing God and making a mistake. Then he hung up.

That was it, I thought.

Three months later I decided to give him a call, just to see how he was doing. I called the church early in the morning. The receptionist answered. I asked for the pastor...and she told me he was no longer there.

Silence.

I asked, "Well, where is he?" She told me that he had left and wouldn't be returning.

I found out later he'd been having an affair with *two women* in the church (both in the choir) *at the same time*. The church was falling apart...

I guess God knew. No, I *know* God knew. He protected us. I'm glad we didn't move our whole family right into the middle of that situation. Even though it looked so perfect, my unknown future was in the hands of the all-knowing God.

Proverbs 16:25 says, "There is a way that seems right to a man, but its end is the way of death" (ESV).

Without a doubt, one of the most powerful forms of agreement is between a husband and wife. I am thankful that we both found ourselves on the same page regarding this church position. It allowed us to stand together against a wrong decision. A decision that was not just about a job, but a bad situation overall.

I've always tried to follow after God's peace. And this situation was no exception. Neither one of us could find peace about accepting this offer. We knew the safest place in all the world is in the middle of the will of God.

No matter how things look right now, know that God is still in control of your life. Stay in peace and obey Him, and believe that He will always guide you in the right direction.

"When I'm worried, it's because I'm trying to do everything myself. When I'm at peace, it's usually because I remember that God is in control" (Unknown). When I put my cares in God's hands, He puts His peace in my heart.

The Bible says to let the peace of God rule in our hearts (Col. 3:15). The Amplified version tells us to let the peace that comes from Christ act as an umpire in our hearts. God's peace can say "safe" to an idea or say "out" to a relationship. Be led by peace. It's always better to miss a few things you should have done than to get into all kinds things you shouldn't.

When God closed the door in California, I knew it was His signal to move forward with our lives together to the next opportunity God had for us. "Blessed is he who trusts in the Lord" (Prov. 16:20).

Although in the short run we were in the same situation, things began to change for the better. Saying *no* freed us to say *yes* to God and some amazing opportunities right around the corner.

It wasn't that long afterward that I wrote my first book and began to speak across the country and internationally.

22 No One Is Sent to Anyone by Accident.

While working at a publishing company, I began to desire to write a book. I had never even remotely considered writing a book until then. I received mostly Bs and Cs in English, while it was my wife, not me, to whom teachers said, "We're going to read books from you someday!"

Yet, I felt strongly I should write a book. So, I did the only thing I knew to do. I bought a book on how to write a book. Not just any book. *The* book, *The Elements of Style.*

After I had read that book, I became entirely convinced I could never do it.

But God had another plan. I decided to go to lunch with a couple I respected from the publishing company. She was over the editorial department, and he was the top information technology person. We met at a favorite Mexican restaurant.

Over chips and salsa, I jumped into the conversation by telling them how I felt I should write a book. I also told them it looked impossible to me. Immediately, they both said I should do it!

I remember the excitement in their voices. They had been in many devotional settings where I had spoken. They told me, "You need to be yourself. You like to tell stories, share short pithy sayings, and encourage everyone. You also don't waste people's time when you speak. Your words are memorable."

Suddenly, I could see how I could do it! Be myself. Be clear. Be short. Be funny. Be encouraging. I started writing. In a little over a year, my first book was completed—*An Enemy Called Average*.

Then God lined up a second person to again change my limited thinking. I'll never forget the day my first book arrived at the office. There it was, all shiny and new...with a decent picture of me on the cover. I took my book into Pat Judd's office. Pat is a good friend. He was about to rock my little world with his words.

I told Pat I had "high expectations" for the book. Even though I knew that the average book published by established publishers sold only around five thousand copies, I was hoping my self-published book would sell the same—maybe even ten thousand!

Pat looked at me and sincerely said, "If this doesn't sell one hundred thousand copies, I'll be disappointed."

Pat was a top executive in book sales and marketing. He knew what he was talking about! Something happened when he spoke those words about my book: a lid flew off! My expectations dramatically changed. Now the sky was no longer the limit. I had known my limits—now I was ignoring them!

I determined to set goals that scared me and excited me at the same time.

The rest is history. That book has sold more than six hundred thousand copies and is printed in numerous languages throughout the world.

I've seen that when God gets ready to bless you, He sends a person (or maybe a married couple) into your life. God blesses people through people.

Spending time with God and with those He connects you to puts everything else in the right perspective.

Words matter. Especially those from the people God sends your way.

What we see depends mainly on what we look for and who we listen to. What I saw was a book I couldn't write, but if I did, one that would moderately sell. God sent people to me to change my perspective and my hope. Something changed. Immediately. Now I could. God set it up for me to talk with individuals who made me see the world and my future differently.

Please believe me when I say the Bible is true when it says, "Now to Him who is able to [carry out His purpose and] do superabundantly more than all that we dare ask or think [infinitely beyond our greatest prayers, hopes, or dreams], according to His power that is at work within us, to Him be the glory in the church and in Christ Jesus throughout all generations forever and ever. Amen" (Eph. 3:20-21 AMP).

Don't downgrade your dream just to fit your reality. Upgrade your belief to match your destiny.

23 The Right Time Is the Right Time.

To everything, there is a season. There is a time for every purpose under heaven. Only you know what season you're in. Only you can know what's inside you.

For some reason, out of the blue, I began to have headaches. These were not migraines, but they were very annoying. I was sensitive to noises and sensitive to music, and the pain would just never go away.

Over time I became concerned about these headaches, so I went to see a neurologist. He cleared me of any major problems, but he also suggested talking to a counselor.

Now, I'd never been to a counselor before for any reason, but these headaches had been going on for months, and they were beginning to get the best of me. So, I decided I would try and talk to a counselor.

I met with a therapist whose name was David. I'll never forget our first meeting. I began to tell him exactly what was going on. He asked some questions, and the meeting lasted forty-five minutes.

I remember thinking, *I can't understand what happened. It seems like we just talked, but I feel a little better.* My counselor told me that we should meet again five more times, so we set up the appointments.

Each one of the counseling sessions followed the same format. We would talk for maybe forty-five minutes, and I would leave. He asked reasonable questions, nothing too invasive or too probing, in my view, but they seemed to be helping me. At the last session, he told me he thought he had a solution that would work for me. The solution? *To do nothing.*

"Do nothing? What do you mean?"

He said, "I mean you need to take some time to do nothing. Go away to a quiet, peaceful place, and do nothing."

I thought, *I could do that. I think so, anyway...*

I came home and told my wife. "Linda, here's what the counselor has suggested, based on all five counseling sessions...that I do nothing."

I made plans to stay in a condo on a small, still, lake down in Florida. I didn't bring my laptop, golf clubs, or anything else—just my clothes and some money for food.

For a week, all I did was sleep, take walks around the pond, and take in an occasional movie. Most importantly, I did *nothing.* I returned from my one week away, and I felt better, but I wasn't completely well. Over time with intentionally taking time off and doing nothing, my headaches went away.

Before I learned to do nothing, I was going ninety miles an hour. God was telling me to slow down, but I wasn't listening. I mean, isn't that what diligent Christians do? I soon realized there was a purpose in my season of resting and waiting.

One of the greatest Bible truths is, to *everything* there is a season.

Respect the season of life that others are in. "Some people come in your life and stay a lifetime and some come for a season, and you will always get yourself in trouble mixing seasonal people up with lifetime expectations" (Tyler Perry as Madea).

Watch out for people who always treat everyone the same and don't respect the season other people find themselves in.

Seasons do change. "God prunes us when He is about to take us into a new season of growth and expansion" (Christine Caine).

Don't let someone else tell you what season you're in. If you do, you'll discover the season they say you're in will probably match their need, not necessarily yours. You'll feel out of season, like you're wearing a bathing suit outside in the middle of winter.

It's OK to say no. No is an anointed word. I give you permission today to say no to those who don't have your best interest at heart. Say no to those who only see in you what they can get out of you, no matter what season you're in.

Don't be in such a rush to get to another season that you miss what God wants you to learn about yourself here and now.

Every next season in your life will demand a different version of you.

Only God can turn a caterpillar into a butterfly and sand into pearls. Embrace the season God has for you.

24 God Is Everywhere and Anywhere You Are.

When I work with authors, I always tell them, "When you publish, anything can happen." *Anything* has happened to me many times.

I was invited to speak in Austria at a publishers' conference, as well as in a church. My friend, Karl Pilsl, pastored the church and was involved in some of the arrangements.

The publishing conference was held at a hotel halfway up a mountain. I remember how beautiful the view was and thinking how treacherous it must be in the winter.

Speaking at this publishing conference was an honor because it was the first conference of its type in Europe. Now that the walls of communism were coming down, those who once published Christian writings in secret were now out in the open, and wanting to learn all they could from American publishers.

I remember noticing a Christian conference going on at the same time in the hotel. I didn't know the person hosting the meetings, but I thought, *How wonderful! A publishing and evangelical conference smack-dab in the middle of Austria. Hitler is surely turning over in his grave!*

I was walking down the hallway to enter the publishing event, when I passed a man going the opposite direction. After we passed each other, I heard a voice behind me asking, "Are you John Mason?" How odd! Who in the world (literally) would know me here?

I turned and said, "Yes, I'm John Mason." The man said he was attending the Christian conference, but he had something to show me. "Follow me to my room!" he exclaimed. He was excited, and I had no clue why. I followed him to his room where he showed me a printout of my entire book, *An Enemy Called Average*, in Bulgarian.

He had translated it from English to Bulgarian and printed it out to take with him on this trip. Then he opened a folder, and in it was a newspaper article. It was an editorial review of my book, picture and all, in the leading newspaper in Bulgaria!

He was so proud. I was shocked. How did he know who I was? How did he translate it? Did he know that what he did was technically illegal? I really didn't care. I was excited my book was reaching into areas where it hadn't been able to go before. I appreciated him and his efforts. I never got a copy of that book, though.

God can find you, wherever, whenever. "When I wake up, you are still with me" (Ps. 139:18 NLT). He certainly was there directing the man in the hallway that morning in Austria.

Stop every day and look at the size of God. The Bible tells us that the eyes of the Lord are roaming throughout the whole earth, so that He can show Himself strong on behalf of people whose hearts are completely His.

The Lord finds us where we are, and, with our obedience, will take us where we ought to go. "Nearness to God brings likeness to God. The more you see God, the more of God will be seen in you" (Charles Spurgeon).

"The Lord is near to all who call upon Him" (Ps.145:18). He is not a distant God. In fact, you are as close to God as you choose to be. So, every day do something that will lead you closer to Him.

God shows He's near to us in every book of the Bible. Realize God has all of us in His sight and in His hands. He's there when you draw near to Him in prayer and in praise. He's right there when we're at our best and when we're at our worst. Reach out to Him today.

Nothing can separate you from God and His relentless love for you (see Romans 8:38-39). Bad things can't, and neither can tall mountains and meetings halfway around the world.

25 Don't Believe Everything You Think.

The tragedy that occurred on September 11, 2001, is a day that people will remember their whole lives. In fact, most of us can say exactly where we were when we heard of the Twin Towers falling.

I was scheduled to speak in Buffalo, New York, about two weeks after September 11. Anyone who flew during that time remembers how different the airport experience was. I distinctly remember my first flight after that terrorist attack—you may be able to as well.

I was flying from Tulsa to Chicago, then connecting to another flight on my way to Buffalo. There were armed officers everywhere at the O'Hare International Airport in Chicago. Machine guns were present and security quadrupled. Every flyer was much more tense than usual. Fortunately, my flight from Tulsa to Chicago was uneventful.

I had determined that I was going to preach on fear as my message that Sunday morning, and I was mulling over some of the points I wanted to make. Little did I know I was about to obtain some more material that I completely didn't expect! I boarded my flight to Chicago from Buffalo. Because I was traveling a lot at that time, I had received a complimentary upgrade to first class. I remember sitting in my aisle seat as passengers boarded the plane. The atmosphere in the aircraft was very different. People were quiet and nervous.

Nearly all the passengers had boarded the plane when a single man of Middle Eastern descent in his twenties boarded the plane carrying a duffel bag. Immediately people began to mumble, "Who is this person? Why is he on this flight?" After only a couple more passengers boarded, three other Middle Eastern men in their twenties followed them in, looking quite like the 9/11 terrorists.

Conversations were now going on amongst all the passengers in first class, some even saying out loud, "Let's get those people off this plane."

Then a German Shepherd-sounding dog began to bark very loudly in the baggage area under the plane. *Was something loaded onto this plane that shouldn't be here?* we wondered, exchanging glances.

I began to feel the fear I was about to preach about the next morning. It was intense, the atmosphere thick with it. Unexpectedly, four officials from American Airlines boarded the plane and met with the pilot. They weren't gate agents; they were administrative types and were having what looked like a serious conversation.

My mind was racing. I was thinking of my family back home and wondering if this was my last day on earth.

After about ten minutes in the cockpit, the four officials left the plane. The flight attendant shut and locked the door. We taxied out and took off. To make matters worse, it was nighttime. I was wondering, *How long before the bomb goes off!* At that point, I'd completely forgotten that I was preaching about fear and worry in about twelve hours.

Of course, as you know since you're reading this book, we landed safely in Buffalo. No crash, no explosion, only fear robbing me of my peace. That Sunday morning service, I confessed I was now, even more, an authority on fear and shared my experience on the plane. I'm sure my conviction was stronger than ever.

Fear is the misuse of God's creative imagination that He put inside each one of us. Think about how creative we can be with our fears. A hangnail can go from an annoyance to a full-blown amputation in a matter of minutes if we let worry take over our imaginations.

Fear tricks us into living stagnant lives. Don't let it paralyze you. The fears we don't face become our limits. Don't let your fear of what could happen, make nothing happen.

Worry kills more dreams than failure ever will. Don't let it decide your future. Whatever your desire is, you must want it more than you're afraid of it.

The popular saying is true: *everything* you want is on the other side of your fears. "The cave you fear to enter holds the treasure you seek" Joseph Campbell).

Set goals that scare you and excite you at the same time. Inhale courage. Exhale fear.

Hope and fear can't occupy the same space at the same time. That's why we should follow this Scripture: "Casting down imaginations, and every high thing that exalts itself against the knowledge of God, and bringing into captivity every thought to the obedience of Christ" (2 Cor. 10:5 AKJV).

Fear is like fog. When the sun (Son) shows up, it goes away. "I trust in God, so why should I be afraid?" (Ps. 56:4 NLT).

You have two choices concerning your future...fear or faith. Like the choice little Billy had.

> A pastor asked little Billy if he said his prayers every night.
>
> "Yes sir," the boy replied.
>
> "And do you always say them in the morning, too?" the pastor asked.
>
> "No sir," Billy replied. "I'm not scared in the daytime" (Unknown).

Each of us has a choice—we can be positive or negative. Faith-filled or fear-filled.

The phrase "do not be afraid" is written in the Bible three hundred sixty-five times. That's a daily reminder from God to live fearless every day.

26 God Is at Work When You Least Expect It.

I was starting my first week at college. I had enrolled in freshman English, like all the rest of my class. It was an early-morning class, so each student was slowly trying to find a seat.

I spotted a cute brunette and decided to sit next to her. I hadn't yet bought my syllabus for the class. She, however, had happened to obtain two syllabi for the class (who gets two?).

Perfect!

When she discovered I didn't have a syllabus, she happily gave me her extra. It wasn't long after when I asked her out on a date. I've been dating her ever since. That beautiful girl is my wife, Linda. This story is also the perfect reflection of our relationship: she with two syllabi and I with none.

You can meet thousands of people without any of them really touching you. And then you meet one person, and your life is changed forever.

It's wonderful to know that God is working on our behalf even when we least expect to see it!

As I was writing this, I realized I was thinking of Linda, and I began to wonder how long she'd been on my mind. Then it occurred to me: since I met her, she's never left it.

Imagine a year from now and realize, that today, God is already working on your behalf. He knows the end from the beginning. And the beginning from the end. Just because something hasn't worked out for you now, doesn't mean there's not something big in store for you in the future.

We spend our whole lives worrying about the future, planning for the future, trying to predict the future, as if figuring it out will cushion the blow. But the future is always changing. We don't have to know everything today. We just need to trust Him with our future.

The future is the home of our deepest fears and wildest hopes. But one thing is sure—when it finally reveals itself, it's never the way we imagined it.

The best thing about the past is that it shows you what not to bring into the future. And just because the past didn't turn out like you wanted it to, doesn't mean your future can't be better than you ever imagined.

Corrie ten Boom said, "Never be afraid to trust an unknown future to a known God." What a wonderful thought it is that some of the best days of our lives haven't yet happened.

27 Nothing Is as It Appears. Nothing.

On many occasions, I've had the privilege to speak at an excellent "Increase Conference" in Hawaii that's hosted by Bob Harrison. I know what you're thinking—"suffering for Jesus," right? These events are held at beautiful resorts right on the ocean in Kauai, Maui, or the Big Island. I have a very good time, and my wife, Linda, always wants to come along, which makes it even better.

One time we were staying on the Big Island at a hotel that was exceptionally beautiful and popular to tourists, not only from the United States, but also from Japan. The décor reflected popular art, statues, and structures from both cultures. There were many tasteful Buddha statues, along with lots of American landscaping and furnishings.

One unusually hot day I was sitting out at the pool. Being a rotund person with only a few hairs left on top of my head, I found myself sitting cross-legged, shirt off, in the shaded section. After only a few minutes, I noticed a group of six Asian couples looking at me, pointing their fingers my way, and talking amongst themselves.

Only a minute or two later, they all began to walk solemnly toward me. As they arrived in front of me, each one slowly bowed down and started to worship me.

OK, I'm kidding. This didn't happen.

Every time in Hawaii when this "Buddha-body-boy" tells this story the crowd pauses, then lets out a big laugh. So, I couldn't resist sharing it with you.

What you see isn't always what you get. Life is full of opposites, and so is the Bible. In fact, I believe one of the primary reasons the Bible was written was to teach us to expect the opposite. Faith in place of fear. Peace replacing confusion. Health taking the place of sickness. God's light instead of darkness.

Furthermore, we're instructed to be humble, then we'll be exalted; show mercy, then watch mercy come to us; give, and it will be given to us; be weak to become strong; serve to become a leader; and be last to be first. Opposites.

Calvin Coolidge said, "We do not need more intellectual power, we need more moral power.... We do not need more of the things that are seen; we need more of the things that are unseen."

What is unseen is more real than what is seen. Look beyond what you see and on the lookout to "see the unseen" in your life. Our invisible God and the Holy Spirit are at work in your life.

28 Better Things Are Coming.

I'm a former high school basketball coach. I know people who meet me in person don't automatically think, *He coached basketball.*

Despite being vertically challenged, I loved coaching basketball. And for a long time, I thought I would even make a career out of it. I felt very natural doing it. Because the private Christian school where I coached was not a member of the state athletic association, we could do pretty much what we wanted.

For four years I was an assistant coach, and we had a typical schedule of playing only other Christian schools. But when I became the head coach, I signed our team up for seven different tournaments, and scheduled as many public schools as I could. We played a forty-two-game schedule...winning 75 percent of them!

I had kids from all around town wanting to play for me, and I found myself in their homes talking to their moms and dads about coming to the school. It was crazy. My arrangement with the school was only as a coach. I didn't teach. For me, that was perfect.

My assistant coach was also the athletic director. He had never coached basketball before, but he did the best he could. I was doing all I could to develop a stellar basketball program and grow as a coach.

After my second successful season, I set up a full summer league schedule as a team for the first time, started an off-season conditioning program, and persuaded a former NBA player to be a volunteer coach. I went to a top-flight coaches' clinic and was looking forward to another great season.

A couple of days before school was scheduled to begin, I received a call from the school's superintendent requesting a meeting. As I walked into his office, I could tell something was up. He had a strange look in his eye. With trembling voice, he said that I was not going to be coaching basketball that upcoming season. He said my assistant coach, who was also the athletic director, had come to him and stated that *God had told him he was supposed to be the head coach.*

Flabbergasted, I was hurt, angry, and confused. My assistant had never coached before. I understood, better than anyone, how little he knew. I also knew that every assistant coach in America "hears a voice" telling them they can and should be the head coach. That doesn't make it God's voice, and it certainly doesn't make it true.

I told the superintendent this was a mistake. His only response was, "God said that to him, and we didn't know that you wanted to come back." Really? I'd been their head coach for two years, and had just finished coaching the team that summer in a public-school-sponsored league and started an active off-season player conditioning program. There was no question the program was successful and moving in the right direction.

I said I was going to talk with the pastor (his boss) about this. I left the office, stunned.

The meeting with the pastor began by him thanking me for coaching, then he repeated the assistant coach's "God told him he was to be the head coach" line. I said, "Every assistant coach in America hears that voice!" But he wasn't listening to any of it.

I finally told him, "I feel like leaving this church, but I'm not going to." (I believe in running *to* something, not *from* something). Leaving offended is not what I want to do.

The pastor said, "If we did make a mistake, we will admit it to you, and we'll bring you back." I said OK and left, but I knew in my heart it was over.

The season started in November. By December they were already interviewing new coaches. By February they had hired another coach who was also a full-time teacher. I never heard a word from anyone.

I'm sure there was no ill intent from anyone at the school, the pastor, or my assistant coach. In fact, my relationship with them continued to be good for many years afterward.

What is most important to know is this: when things happen that are beyond *your* control, it doesn't mean that *God* is not in control.

The bottom line is this: people will do what they want to do. They will hear what they want to hear, and see what they want to see. At the end of the day, God is in control, even when a person tries to get in the way.

I never coached at a high school again. But God was still working on my behalf, even if men were not. The Lord connected me later that year with the father of one of the boys I coached. That relationship took me directly to the publishing world where I would learn to help authors and to write books. Because I coached basketball, I found my highest calling outside of basketball.

Proverbs 19:21 says, “You can make many plans, but the Lord’s purpose will prevail (NLT).

Many times, God puts us on (or takes us off) a path to bring us somewhere completely different than we expect. Remember, He is in control…no matter what people do. He will get you to where He wants you to be “in due season,” if you won’t give up.

His plans will always be greater and more beautiful than ours. Sometimes, you’re not given what you want because something better is planned for you instead.

God closes doors because it’s time to *move* forward. He knows you probably won’t move unless your circumstances force you to. Trust the transition.

Here’s what I do. Accept what is. Let go of what was. And have trust in God with what will be.

Later, I did have the privilege of coaching my youngest son David’s basketball teams as he grew up. He went on to play Division I college basketball!

“Where you are today is no accident. God is using the situation you are in right now to shape you and prepare you for the place He wants to bring you into tomorrow. Trust Him with His plan even if you don’t understand it” (Unknown).

So pray this: Dear God, if today I lose my hope, please remind me that Your plans are better than my loftiest dream.

You may not always understand why God allows things to happen, but you can be certain He’s not making any mistakes. God’s way is way better than your own. His plan is bigger than your plans. His dream for your life is more rewarding, more fulfilling, better than you have ever dreamed of. Now stay open and let God do it His way.

29 Each Person You Serve Is Jesus in Disguise.

—Mother Teresa, paraphrased

People matter to God.

I was excited and nervous. I had been invited to speak at a large church for their Sunday-night service. There would be several thousand people there, and I already knew what I felt I should share.

I was honored to be invited and was looking forward to that evening's service. I was already in town, so I attended the Sunday-morning service. The service went forward as usual—singing, announcements, and offering. Before the sermon began, the pastor announced that this Sunday (the second Sunday of the month) was "missionary Sunday." We would be taking up a second offering for our missionaries. *OK*, I thought, *that's good.* I remember making a second donation.

As that collection ended, a man walked up front and began to describe a special need within the church. It was a worthy cause, a much-needed area of ministry. As he finished, we heard another announcement that there would be a special offering for that area, too. The buckets were passed for the third time. I don't remember if I gave. I do remember feeling a little uneasy.

Finally, Sunday night arrived. I was ready. The service began, and it was a wonderful time of worship and singing. Then it was offering time...

Yes, what happened in the morning service was repeated in the evening service. Three more offerings! I knew that most people who were there that night had been there that morning. They were asked to give six times!

I gave my message, and it was well received. Thank God.

As I was returning to my seat, the congregation was informed a special offering would be taken up for me. One, two, three, four, five, six, seven times these dear people would be asked to give this day! I was embarrassed. I wanted to say, "Forget it," but I didn't. The buckets were already being passed—again.

I'm not saying what happened was *wrong*, but it certainly wasn't *right*. I'm thankful for opportunities to give to God's work. But sometimes too much of a good thing is way too much.

People are not a means to an end. People are the end. Each and every one of them matters to God.

You and I might not ask for seven offerings from those we work and live with every day, but I think we can all treat others better. Everywhere we go, let's look at each other not as a means, but more as the end.

"Rudeness is the weak man's imitation of strength" (Eric Hoffer). Never take advantage of someone. We all reap what we sow: sow mercy, and we'll receive mercy; sow generosity, and people will be generous back to us. Sow a smile, and watch how you light up another person's life!

Be kind when possible...it's always possible.

See people as God sees them and don't judge them by what they wear, where they live, what they drive, or how they speak. It's God's idea to care for people regardless of what they can give back to us. Everyone deserves respect and kindness.

If you truly love others, you'll want what's best for them; whether that includes you or not. How you make others feel about themselves says a lot about you. "We rise by lifting others" (Robert Ingersoll).

If you can be one thing in life, be kind. What means most in life is what you have done for others. Most people can smile for two months on five words of praise and a pat on the back. Kindness doesn't cost a dime. Sprinkle it everywhere.

Build others up. Put their insecurities to rest. Remind them they're worthy. Tell them they are incredible. Be a light in their darkness.

Put others first. No one is more deceived or cheated than a selfish person. You and I were created to help others.

I love it when I have the opportunity to speak, whether it's in a church or business setting. I almost always say to myself afterward, *This is why I was created* and *I want to do this more.* I think the basis for this feeling is that long ago, I realized I was there for the audience, not the audience there for me.

When I prepare to speak somewhere, and when I'm there, I am careful to remind myself that I am there to serve others. In fact, my usual prayer is this: "Lord, I'm the lowest in the room, I'm here as a servant. Use me however You want to bless and encourage Your people."

"When you realize God's purpose for your life isn't just about you, He will use you in a mighty way" (Dr. Tony Evans).

There are two types of people in the world: those who come into a room and say, “Here I am!” and those who say, “Ah, there you are!” How do you know a good person? A good person makes others good. Find happiness by helping others find it.

Satisfaction means we go to sleep at night knowing our talents and gifts were used in a way that served others. No matter how educated, talented, rich, or cool you believe you are, how you treat people ultimately tells all.

Never think that what you have to offer is insignificant. There will always be someone out there who needs what you have to give. “You’ll never be happy if you chase money and stuff all of your life, but you can find true joy through giving and serving others” (Dave Ramsey).

“There comes a point in your life when you realize who matters, who never did, who won’t anymore, and who always will. And in the end, you learn who is fake, who is true, and who would risk it all for you” (Unknown).

Be *that* person, the one who puts others before yourself.

30 Your Success Begins Where Most Others Quit.

Never ever give up on what you know you should do. Ninety-seven percent of the people who stopped too soon are employed by the 3 percent who never gave up. Many of the world's great failures did not realize how close they were to success when they gave up.

Galatians 6:9 says, "Let us not become weary in doing good, for at the proper time we will reap a harvest if we do not give up" (NIV). Is it that simple? Yes!

Here's my challenge to you today: become famous for completing important, challenging tasks. I promise you this: you will be shocked at the impact of your persistence.

More than twenty years ago, I remember feeling led to write. I didn't know what to do. I knew over a thousand new books were published each day, and that most of them were never read.

When I was in college if you had asked me to list fifty things I would do, writing a book wouldn't have been one of them. But I started...and I worked at it for nearly two years.

I had no built-in audience, no As in English. But I did have the determination and a commitment to finish. After almost two years,

I'll never forget at 4:30 in the morning typing the last word into my Apple IIC computer (128K), falling into my bed, and sobbing for quite a while...it was finished! *An Enemy Called Average.*

Little did I know that more than a half-million people were about to read this book in thirty-seven languages around the world.

Recently I was pondering how good God has been to me about the sales of my book. I was blown away when I realized, if you took the number of books this individual book sold, and laid one book down every mile at the equator, it would encircle the earth twenty-four times. Wow! God is good, and He sure does have "the whole world in His hands."

You will be shocked at the impact of your persistence!

"Difficult roads often lead to beautiful destinations" (Unknown). "Never give up on something that you can't go a day without thinking about" (Winston Churchill).

Coca-Cola only sold twenty-five bottles its first year. Every start-up begins with zero customers, zero sales, and zero profits.

The only way to succeed is to never give up. And never give up without a fight. Giving up on your goal because of one setback is like slashing your three good tires because one goes flat.

Luke 18:1 says to "always pray and never give up" (NLT). Every time you feel like quitting, think about why you began. Be relentless in the pursuit of what sets your heart on fire.

"It's impossible," said pride.
"It's risky," said experience.
"It's pointless," said reason.
"Give it a try," whispered the heart (Unknown).

The moment you're ready to quit is usually the moment right before a miracle happens. So, don't give up!

31 Be Thankful for What You *Don't* Get.

If you can't be satisfied with what you've reached, at least be thankful for what you've escaped.

I like to go away when I write. I usually go to some warm resort-type place (like the one I'm at now) and work for many days straight, barely coming out, unless it's to play a little golf.

But one time I decided to stay at a nice hotel in my hometown to write.

I left there to head out to dinner, and as I drove, I was completely absorbed in thoughts about my latest book—so focused that I drove right through a red light at one of the busiest intersections in my city!

I was jarred out of thinking about my book when I was greeted by several horns, and one man who wanted to let me know "I was number one" with his finger. Shaken, I pulled into a parking lot to give thanks to God for His protection—even when I'm stupid.

We all have a lot to be thankful for. *Yes, we all have a lot to be thankful for!*

Start each day you're given with thanks. Gratitude positions us rightly before God. How grateful you are is a sure indicator of your spiritual health. The more gratitude you have, the healthier you are.

Clearly, gratitude reveals the depth of our relationship with God. I try to say thank you more often than "Lord, can You?"

Thankfulness has an incredible capacity to simplify our lives. It brings a clear, concise perspective.

You will find yourself more full of hope when you view things through the lens of gratitude.

PART III

Be Free

32 Color Outside the Lines.

I wasn't afraid of being different. I was afraid of being the same as everyone else.

When I wrote my first book, *An Enemy Called Average*, I knew I needed to make my book stand out and not blend in. As an unknown author with no platform, I faced an uphill battle making my book known to the masses.

Since I was experienced in publishing, I should have had an advantage. But I was unsure what that advantage was exactly...

I always hated (and still do) having to read twenty pages to get one point. I know some people enjoy being drawn into the beautiful details of illustrious writing, but I find it boring. I'm impatient.

So, I decided to do something no one else was doing at the time—write two-page chapters. That was about how long my interest held, and I figured that was true for a lot of other people, too. People could read four chapters and feel very proud (but they only had to read eight pages)! Plus, it forced me to make every word count. I remember trying to make each sentence stand on its own.

Thousands of people have told me they bought my books because of the short chapters. Probably the most hilarious comment I get is when people tell me they read my books in their bathroom! An embarrassed smile usually follows (from them and me). Many times, I can't help but respond, "I'm not surprised. Each nugget chapter is just the right length...and quite moving!"

I did a second thing that was almost sacrilegious...I didn't bold-face the Scriptures in my book. Books at that time always did that to make the Scripture stand out. But I knew that most people skipped the Scriptures in books, especially long ones or verses they already knew. Instead, (watch out for lightning!) I chose to bold-face my best one-liners. I wanted to highlight my best thoughts as people flipped through my book in stores so they could see that the book offered some compelling expressions. Instead of bold-facing the Scriptures, I decided to italicize them, still highlighting and differentiating them from my own thoughts.

Of course, I was criticized. "Your book is a mile wide, and an inch deep," said one church leader. "You're elevating your thoughts above the Bible." I welcomed the critics. I was standing out, and my writing style was helping people read and then tell others.

I knew that 70 percent of all books are never read. I wanted to write a book people would read!

"Learn the rules like a pro, so you can break them like an artist" (Pablo Picasso). To be a success, you must stand out, not blend in. You must be odd to be number 1.

Break the rules more often and you'll gain a huge advantage over those too afraid to risk it. Take advantage of everyone's natural desire to conform.

If you don't fit in you're probably doing the right thing. See your difference as a strength. Be humble enough to know you're not better than everyone else, and wise enough to know that you're different from the rest.

"I want to stand as close to the edge as I can without going over. Out on the edge, you see all the kinds of things you can't see from the center" (Kurt Vonnegut).

You will never influence the world by trying to be like it. Make a deliberate choice to be different.

33 Question Everything.

I love to ask questions. I'll admit, it drives my wife crazy sometimes—question after question after question. I've even written two books about questions, *Ask* and *Why Ask Why.*

Have you found yourself in a situation where you don't feel the freedom to ask a question? An environment where the very action of asking makes people think that you doubt or you're not "on the team"?

"Questions are only offensive to those who have something to hide" (Gary Hopkins).

A right question can change the direction of your life.

I'm glad I knew the right question to ask.

While a senior in high school, I was offered a four-year, full-tuition scholarship to attend a prestigious college in Indiana. It was an honor to be offered such an excellent opportunity.

At the same time, I had applied to another school; this one in another state at a Christian university. I had visited on a college weekend, where I remember feeling a closeness to God that I had never felt before. It was a new university and on the rise. It was a long way from home, but I was excited about the possibility. The bad news was they were offering me zero scholarships, and I hadn't even been accepted.

The college in Indiana also invited me to their college weekend—a day or two in the dorm/fraternity, extensive campus tours, and a persuasive presentation about why they were the very best school in the state. They were recruiting me, like an athlete. It was a beautiful campus with first-class academics. And it was *free.* Over the weekend, I noticed they had beer machines in the hallways, girls everywhere in the dorms, and rumor had it...strippers coming in.

I remember walking alone on that campus thinking, *Should I go here or not?* As I pondered my future choice, a question came to me that would eventually change my life.

I asked myself, *What kind of a person am I going to be four years from now if I go here, or to the Christian university?* The moment I asked that question, the answer became apparent.

I want to affirm that God calls people to secular schools, but in my case, I knew, *based on my question*, where I should go. I chose the Christian one.

The answer to that question was a defining moment in my life. I met my wife, established lifelong friends, and learned about God in a way I never would have at my other choice.

Questions are powerful. Unfortunately, many leaders and organizations discourage them. Never find yourself attached to or a part of something that discourages or doesn't allow questions. It's a bad sign if you can't ask questions. Questions bring growth.

Is the truth afraid of the questions? No, truth welcomes questions. They bring answers and freedom.

If you go to an elementary school, you will find a class full of questions. They might ask, "Why is the sky blue? Why do we have ten fingers and toes? Why can't birds talk, but I hear them singing? Why don't I have eyes in the back of my head like I hear people say?" They ask insightful, probing questions. If you talk to most middle-aged people, you won't find that! They've become incurious. They've lost something from their childhood.

"He who asks a question is a fool for five minutes; he who does not ask a question remains a fool forever" (Chinese Proverb).

"The way you become world-class is...by asking good questions" (Tim Ferriss).

34 Have Fun! (Seriously.)

Years ago, I was presented with an interesting opportunity to be a substitute teacher for several weeks. I was looking forward to it. I had decided ahead of time I would follow the specific curriculum they asked of me, but I was going to present it in a much more interesting, entertaining, and fun way. I was hopeful that the students and I would enjoy the experience.

I thought things were going well…until I had an encounter with the assistant principal. I was walking down the hall when I heard a voice from behind me saying, "Mr. Mason, I need to talk to you, now." She came right up beside me, looked me straight in the eye and said, "We have a problem. The kids are having too much fun in your class, and we don't have fun here at this school."

I wanted to ask her, "Is what you believe so fragile, so ineffective, that you can't enjoy life with a smile?" But I didn't.

What I knew, that she obviously didn't, is that it's OK to enjoy life. It's OK to have fun, to smile, to laugh, and to have a good time.

A grim countenance does not equal a more spiritual experience. I try to follow this philosophy of life; I want to hire a person who whistles while they work. I like to sing at the office, even though it's mostly a joyful "noise."

My wife, Linda, and I laugh every day. Even in the most challenging of situations, we have found ourselves laughing. I remember right after I had heart surgery (yes, the kind where they open your chest) having to ask her to leave my hospital room several times because being around each other was causing us to laugh—and every single laugh was causing a great deal of pain right in the middle of my chest. We have the kind of relationship where we can sit around doing nothing but still have fun because we're together.

The old saying is true; if you can laugh at it, you can live with it. You know your life needs to change when someone asks you what you do for fun, and you can't even remember the last time you had fun.

Life is to be enjoyed, not endured. The truth is, "People rarely succeed unless they have fun in what they are doing" (Dale Carnegie).

There's nothing spiritual about not having fun. You don't always need a logical or biblical reason for doing everything in your life.

When you're having fun, you're making memories. Life only comes around once. So why not do what makes you happy and be around people who make you smile?

I smile at what Mark Twain said, "Forgive quickly, kiss slowly. Love truly. Laugh uncontrollably."

35 Denying the Truth Doesn't Change the Facts.

More people would learn from their problems if they weren't so busy denying them.

I made a phone call to a friend I knew wasn't doing very well. I started our conversation by asking him, "How are you doing, Leon?"

He began to talk in a preprogrammed kind of way, saying, "Everything is super good! I'm blessed beyond measure! Things are fantastic!"

I let him finish.

Then I asked him (again), "Leon, how are you *really* doing?" He quietly said, "Not so good."

"How can I help?" I responded. Now we were making progress.

Denying a problem doesn't make it go away. It usually only makes it worse. How can you fix something if you don't know, or admit, what's wrong?

Unfortunately, in many Christian environments, we're not allowed—or supposed to have—problems.

This mind-set has become a doctrine of denial.

Sometimes leaders are the worst at this. The problem with this theology is that now the only thing they can talk about are their successes. They can't talk about their problems because talking about them would question the fact that there is always victory.

As a result, you tend to hear leaders only talk about their high points, which creates a distorted image—a unique breed of supermen and superwomen with supernatural powers. They're never discouraged, never have trouble, never have anything wrong with them. They become legends...inaccurate ones.

What are we going to do with our problems if we're not supposed to have any? How are we going to solve our problems if we're not allowed to admit we have them?

What you can't say owns you. What you hide controls you.

The freest person in the world is the one who has nothing to hide. Don't be fooled. People aren't what they "post" themselves to be. "You can speak with spiritual eloquence, pray in public, and maintain a holy appearance...but it is your behavior that will reveal your true character" (Dr. Steve Maraboli).

Denying the facts does not make them go away. Saying something is super good when in truth it's super bad is simply not telling the truth.

Denying the bone is sticking out does not heal the compound fracture in your arm. The "doctrine of denial" is empty, and walking by *fake* not *faith*, never works. In fact, these kinds of ideas can lead to dishonesty, deception, fraud, and lying.

Denying a problem never helps solve it. The truth always comes out in the end, no matter how hard anyone tries to hide it or stop it. Denial is just a temporary delay to the inevitable; in the worst cases, an angry disappointment with God based on inaccurate belief.

The truth is the truth, even if no one says it. A lie is a lie, even if everyone believes it.

You should always be able to tell your husband or wife exactly how you feel about everything. And be honest with God; besides, He already knows what you're thinking.

Sometimes you can tell more about a person by what they hide than by what is shown. Not telling me something or hiding something on purpose is just the same as lying.

You and I are to walk by faith, not by *fake*. Honesty is always the best policy. How can we help others without it? How can we confess our faults to one another if everyone says they don't have any problems?

36 You Don't Need a Reason to Help People.

Unfortunately, I found myself on a church board trying to deal with the moral failure of its leader. As he and his wife began to navigate his restoration and the rebuilding of their marriage, I remember a conversation I had with him about where he found himself.

"I am fully responsible for my actions," he quietly said to me. "I am going back to the basics, back to my first love in my relationship with God."

As we continued to talk, he said, "What is revealing to me is how many people are completely gone from our lives. There are hardly any relationships left—even the six fellow pastors responsible for my restoration. Not one has contacted me." I remember looking at him and saying, "Jim (not his real name), you're not worth the risk to them."

Jesus hung out with people like Jim. He took risks with tax collectors, prostitutes, and Gentiles. I believe that's where He most wanted to be.

It's the sick who need a physician. Don't we all need the loving, healing touch of the Great Physician?

God sends people into our lives that we're supposed to take risks on—people others run from or ignore.

Sherman (not his real name) was someone no one had anything to do with at high school. He was an awkward young man. Intellectually slow, he was always disheveled. His hair was never combed and was littered with dandruff. And he always smelled—in a way that you remembered. He lived alone with his mother in a run-down old farmhouse.

Sherm, as I called him, became my friend. I don't know why I gravitated toward him. There were plenty of other odd kids in school I stayed away from. But Sherm was someone I wanted to be friends with. I knew he needed a friend.

Some days, I would pick him up for school and bring him home afterward. I'd buy him pizza, take him to school events. And one time, I managed to arrange a double date for him and me. I talked to him about the Lord and knew he had a personal relationship with God.

Sherm was always quiet. I guess in the kind of way outcasts can be. He wanted to be liked, just like all of us do (especially in high school). I knew my friendship meant a lot to him. But what he did for me touched me more than anything I ever did for him.

I saw how blessed I was, and how everyone—*everyone*—matters to God. I felt assigned to him, and in a divine way, he was assigned to me during our high school years.

I lost track of Sherm as I moved eight hundred miles away to college. I heard he got a job and was working the best he could. I've never forgotten his impact on my life perspective.

I believe God sends people across our path not just to be a blessing to us, but more importantly so we can be a blessing to them.

I challenge you to pray this life-changing, dangerous (in a good way) prayer. "Lord, send those into my life I can bless. Show me how to love them as You love them. And may they come to know You because I loved them too."

A good deed bears interest. I believe that one of the marks of true greatness is to develop greatness in others.

I have found that outstanding people have a unique perspective. That perspective is that greatness is not deposited into them to stay, but rather to flow through them into others.

Whatever we praise, we increase. Share some hope and encouragement with others.

Your opportunity may not look or act like Sherm. But, I know each and every one of us has people in our lives we can help. There is no investment you can make that will pay you so well as investing in the improvement of others throughout your life.

37 Real Lessons Follow Stories with Lots of Ups and Downs.

Let me tell you two stories. One true, the other legendary.

Zingo was a famous local roller coaster where we live. It featured nearly a ninety-foot drop and fifty-mile-per-hour speed. It was built by hand in 1968 and constructed out of wood and steel. The wood made it feel a little rickety, which added to the frightfulness of the ride.

It was a good, fast, roller coaster.

My daughter, Michelle, was eight years old at the time and had been asking me for months to take her on the Zingo, now that she was just tall enough to ride it. I wasn't sure how it would go, but I said yes and off we went to Bell's Amusement Park where the Zingo awaited us.

Excited, we stood in line waiting our turn, watching each group of nearly all young people ride the coaster. Some screamed, others closed their eyes, but most were having a great time.

Finally, it was our turn. We got into our seat, the very front one. The attendant "locked" us in by lowering a bar in front of us.

There was so much space between Michelle and the bar that she couldn't reach it. And there was an opening to her right, where we had entered our seats. I saw her initial fright, so I put my arm around her. Off we slowly went, up the first climb.

I had ridden the Zingo before and knew the first drop was the biggest, so I looked over at Michelle to see how she was doing. Her eyes were fixed, her arms wrapped around me in a death grip.

To add to the thrill, the designers of the ride added a click, click, click to each foot or two as we slowly moved skyward.

About three-quarters of the way up, Michelle's fear transformed into a full, female scream...and we weren't even at the top yet. In a few seconds, we would drop nearly ninety feet at fifty miles per hour!

Thinking she was about to be flung from her seat, a certain death, she held me even tighter and screamed louder. She continued screaming from the first drop until the moment we *finally* ground to a halt, back where we started. Alive, but in my case, with diminished hearing in the ear closest to her (not really).

This is a memory Michelle and I will never forget.

An elderly Florida lady did her shopping, and upon returning to her car, found four males in the act of leaving with her vehicle.

She dropped her shopping bags and drew her handgun, proceeding to scream at the top of her voice, "I have a gun, and I know how to use it! Get out of the car!"

The four men didn't wait for a second invitation. They got out and ran like mad. The lady, somewhat shaken, then proceeded to load her shopping bags into the back of the car and get into the driver's seat. She was so shaken that she could not get her key into the ignition. She tried and tried, and then it dawned on her why.

A few minutes later she found her own car parked four or five spaces farther down. She loaded her bags into the car and then drove to the police station. The sergeant to whom she told the story nearly tore himself in two with laughter. He pointed to the other end of the counter, where four pale men were reporting a carjacking by a mad, elderly woman described as white, less than five feet tall, glasses, curly white hair, and carrying a large handgun.

No charges were filed.

The moral of these two stories?

Sometimes, in life, we're the little old lady. We're sure we're right and make everyone react to what we "know" to be true. But maybe we're wrong. That creates havoc, and we need to make it right.

Sometimes, we're the four men. Minding our own business, suddenly surprised to find ourselves ousted from our comfort zone for no apparent reason, only to discover that we were right all along. And then able to go back to what we were doing before—only now with a new perspective and appreciation...along with a smile on our face.

Sometimes we're the ambitious person wanting to ride a "Zingo." We've all been told the best way to overcome our fears is to confront them. And that is true. It's also true that when you get to do something you've always wanted to do, you may be disappointed or even scared once you're there. In any case, you will discover something about yourself you didn't know before.

God expands our horizons every time we turn to Him. The more we get to know God, the more we discover how much more there is to know about Him. He wants to fill every void and every opportunity in our lives.

Life is like a roller coaster. We can either scream every time there's a bump, or we can throw our hands up and enjoy the ride. Through all the twists and turns, ups and downs, our Father is with us from the beginning to the end.

38 Stay Away from Negative People. They Have a Problem for Every Solution.

Once a month, the church I was attending had a men's luncheon. They served a nice buffet, and a speaker shared for twenty minutes before we all went back to work.

At this point in my life, more than thirty years ago, I could only be described as a very unsuccessful person. In fact, if you had told me you wanted to be successful, I would have said to look at my life and do the opposite!

There was a particular luncheon I will never forget that later became a defining moment in my life. I remember eating and listening to the speaker. I don't recall what I ate or what he said. But I do remember what happened next.

I found myself lingering at the restaurant, sitting around a table with five or six other men. I can describe them best as "unproductive Christians." You know the kind of people I'm talking about. The ones who have had four jobs the past two years. The people who are always saying, "God told me this, God said that." Flying off in one direction one month, then another course the next month, and then the complete opposite direction the next month. All talk, no action.

I was hanging out with them way past lunchtime—until a quarter of two in the afternoon! That should tell you how much work I had to do, how diligently I worked, how focused on my priorities I was.

And guess what you would have found us talking about, if you really listened to our words? We were all talking about *why we weren't successful.* I was participating in the conversation right along with everyone else. In fact, I was an authority on that subject.

Suddenly, right in the middle of our conversation, I sensed God speaking to my heart. This is what I heard: *"John, there are some people I don't want you to be around anymore."* And then He gave me their names. He continued, *"There are some people you can be around, but only for a limited amount of time in certain circumstances."* Again, He gave me their names.

What's great about God is that when He takes you out of darkness, He doesn't leave you in the dusk. He brings you into the light.

He continued to speak to my heart. *"There are some people I want you to be around!"* And He gave me three names. These were men who knew me. They saw the gifts and calling in me. They were men who, when I was around them, brought out the best in me, not the worst in me. I was even nicer to my wife after I was around them!

I immediately got up from that table. I remember walking to the southwest corner of the restaurant parking lot. I pointed my finger toward heaven and said, "I'll do it!"

I drove straight home (back then, you had to go there to make phone calls). I picked up the phone, and I called those three men.

I said, "I hope you don't mind, but I need to get together with you on a regular basis." They all said yes.

My life changed!

I noticed a change *that day* as I chose to associate with the right people. For the rest of my life, I've tried to be best friends with those who bring out the best in me (and me in them).

You are only going to be as good as the people you surround yourself with. Be brave enough to let go of those who keep weighing you down.

If, as you read this, names come to you, I encourage you to act. You may need to begin to say no to someone, or invest more time with another. Sometimes the answer to our prayers is a change in our relationships.

If you hang around five confident people, you will be the sixth.
If you hang around five smart people, you will be the sixth.
If you hang around five successful people, you will be the sixth.
If you hang around five idiots, you will be the sixth.

God has right associations for you. You'll know the people who feed your soul, because you'll feel good after spending time with them. Spend time with those who love you unconditionally. Don't waste it on those who only love you when conditions are right.

I'm thankful to the people who walked into my life and made it better. And grateful to the ones who walked out and made it better. God puts people in your life for a reason and removes them from your life for a better reason.

Your best friends are those who bring out the best in you. I love those people I can joke around with and have a lot of fun with, and then have a deep conversation with them and it doesn't feel weird at all.

People think being alone makes you lonely, but I don't think that's true. "Being surrounded by the wrong people is the loneliest thing in the world" (Kim Culbertson).

The less you associate with some people, the more your life will improve. When you remove yourself from unproductive, negative people, good things will start happening for you, and it won't be a coincidence.

Make sure everybody in your "boat" is rowing and not drilling holes when you aren't looking. Think about it...don't many of your sorrows spring out of relationships with the wrong people?

A good friend knows all your stories. A best friend helped you write them. "A true relationship is two imperfect people refusing to give up on each other" (Unknown). Life was meant for good friends and great adventures.

39 Little Things, Little Moments...They Aren't Little!

Have you ever felt belittled when asked, "Are you in *full-time* ministry? Are you traveling to *many* nations? Are you winning *thousands* to the Lord?"

Don't fall into the trap that you matter to God only if you are doing or saying *big* things. "Not all of us can do great things. But we can do small things with great love" (Mother Teresa).

God is in the little things. Everything is important when you're doing God's will. Don't fall into the comparison trap; the trap that says what I'm doing is too small, too unimportant compared to others.

"The way we do small things determines the way we do everything" (Robin Sharma).

Allow yourself small victories. Don't deny giving yourself credit for accomplishing something, no matter how insignificant it might seem at the time. Instead of doing nothing because you're overwhelmed or full of fear, today do something even if it's small because it will be one step closer to your goal.

Small goes where big can't.

Years ago, I was in a hurry. I remember turning off my car but dropping my keys in my quest to get to where I was going.

The problem was, I dropped my keys into the abyss between the seat and the center console. Every driver knows that place—dark, narrow, and hard to navigate. Fortunately for me, my six-year-old son, Mike, was there with me. When I asked him if he could get dad's keys, he willingly stuck his little hand into the spot where I dropped my keys and quickly retrieved them.

His small hand could go where my big hand couldn't. Incidentally, Mike became so good at finding things, that even now as an adult, our family frequently turns to him when we can't find something!

Success is a series of small wins.

Don't despise where you are and what you're doing right now. God starts where you are—always. It's how He takes you from where you are to where He wants you to be.

Everything big starts with something small.

Greatness is a lot of small things done well every day. Do one small thing to make today better than yesterday. "Sometimes the smallest things take up the most room in your heart" (Winnie the Pooh).

"Some believe it is only great power that can hold evil in check, but that is not what I have found. It is the small everyday deeds of ordinary folk that keep the darkness at bay. Small acts of kindness and love" (J.R.R.Tolkien).

If you can't help a hundred people, then help just one. When children fall fifty times as they learn to walk, they never think,

Maybe this isn't for me. No, they keep on taking those small steps...and before long, they're running.

I fell in love with my wife because of the thousand tiny things she never knew she was doing that made me smile. The best portion of your life will be the small, nameless moments you spend smiling and laughing with someone who matters to you. Love is a big thing built of little things.

What looks like a small act to you may be a very big thing to another person. Small daily improvements are the key to staggering, long-term results.

40 You Can Hear for Yourself.

People will eventually show their true colors. So, when someone shows you who they truly are, don't try to paint a different picture.

Not everyone has a right to speak into your life.

"Once upon a time, a beautiful, independent, self-assured princess happened upon a frog in a pond. The frog said to the princess, "I was once a handsome prince until an evil witch put a spell on me. One kiss from you, and I will turn back into a prince. And then we can marry, move into the castle with my mom, and you can prepare my meals, clean my clothes, bear my children, and forever feel happy doing so.

"Later that night, while the princess dined on frog legs, she kept laughing and saying, 'I don't think so'" (Unknown).

I've spent a lot of my adult life as an executive in the publishing world while also as an author. I guess that's like being a director and an actor. Seeing both sides of publishing is enlightening... and frustrating.

I spent some time as the head of a publishing company in Florida. I felt God led me there from Tulsa to help turn the company around. It had floundered for years, and the owner was seriously considering closing it down. Miraculously, God used our team to quickly make the business very profitable.

After nearly three years there, I started to feel my assignment was nearing an end, so I began to consider some other possibilities in publishing. One such opportunity that presented itself was starting a new company with two people I had worked for in publishing before, along with a longtime lawyer friend of mine. This time, I was going to be the president and a 25 percent owner.

My previous employment with these two men had gone well, except for one issue. While I worked for them, I wrote and self-published my first book. They distributed it, and it became one of their top two best-selling books the first year. You might think everyone would be happy about that, but that was not the case, as I would find out.

One year after the book's release and with sales of more than one hundred thousand copies, I was called into a meeting with the general manager, my boss. He said he needed to talk with me about my book. The meeting began with a summary of my sales and a very strange comment. He looked at me and said, "The owner wants you to know that if he had known how well your book would sell, he would not have wanted you to write and publish it." I was stunned and confused at the statement.

He continued, "He feels it's a conflict of interest for you to be an employee here and an author also."

My only amazed response was, "What about all the people who have been helped by my book? Hundreds of thousands!"

He gave no answer to my response.

I also knew they had made a significant profit by distributing my book, with no risk to them. This was all happening at a time when they were in desperate financial need. They had even asked to borrow money from *me* that year to pay an urgent bill!

I thought it was a very strange conclusion, and I saw no negatives for anyone. Yet, they believed what they told me.

Why would I now get in business with this person in starting this new publishing company, if he had a problem with me being an author? It was a good question. And one I was certainly going to ask.

Before I agreed to start this new company, I met with this owner I'd worked for previously. I wanted to know that there was no issue this time with me being an author and involved with him in publishing. He looked me in the eye and told me it was no issue since now I'd be an owner, like him.

So with that issue addressed, we started the company. I left Florida and moved back to Tulsa, now a part owner and president.

Things were moving along well at our new venture. Good authors were showing interest and signing up to do books with us. Then I got a call from my friend the lawyer and partner. He said he needed to come by my house to meet with me *that* night.

That evening he warned me that the next day the two other owners were going to demand I resign and give back all my stock. To say I was shocked was an understatement! The company was only three months old!

I walked into the meeting that next day not knowing what to say or think. Immediately, the previous owner looked at me and said, "We need you to resign, *God told me* you're not supposed to be involved in publishing. We feel it's a conflict for you to be an author and involved in publishing."

Incredulous, I responded, "God hasn't told *me* that!" I knew this man was either lying to my face now or had lied to my face three months before when we started the company. Either way, he was showing his true colors.

I wasn't buying it. I certainly wasn't falling for his line that "God told him." God doesn't speak through people with ulterior motives. And He certainly talks to a person directly first.

But he wasn't budging, neither was the other partner, and all the while my lawyer friend was caught in the middle. I felt I had been played. I had been lied to. I had risked a lot and now was being forced out.

I thought, *How can you lie to a person's face and then use God's name to try and "seal the deal"?* That was dangerous and something I would never consider doing to someone else. (Later, my lawyer friend told me that he had heard him use that same "God told me" line many times on numerous other people.)

Fortunately, my wife, Linda, could see things clearly, and she lovingly talked with me about the right path forward. I'll never forget what she said: "They've shown you their true colors. You shouldn't be in partnership with people like that. We've been delivered! We should celebrate!"

I walked away. It wasn't easy. I saw them prosper without me. I felt alone, but I never, ever doubted I did the right thing. I knew I "worked for my heavenly Father," and I believed He wanted the best for His child.

If you find yourself in the wrong story, close the book and leave.

Knowing when to walk away is wisdom. Being able to is courage. Walking away with your head held high is dignity.

Here's the rest of the story. Later, that publishing company went away and its parent company filed for bankruptcy. They had been close to going under at least two other times. All the stockholders (I would have been one of them) barely escaped losing millions of dollars individually because of having to personally guarantee loans to keep the company going.

Here's a good lesson. Take notice of those who don't celebrate your victories and certainly don't partner with them.

Put God first. Know He will take care of you regardless of man's devices.

Finally, not everyone will want you to succeed. Some people are jealous, dishonest, or greedy. Most importantly, never fall for the line, "God told me" from someone who has ulterior motives. If our loving heavenly Father intends to communicate with you, I guarantee He will (probably many times) try to speak His will to *you* first.

Maybe someone has shown you their true colors. It's time to say no to that relationship. Don't let your loyalty become slavery. "If they don't appreciate what you bring to the table...then let them eat alone" (Avinash Wandre).

Some people come into your life as blessings, and others come into your life as lessons.

I am thankful he showed me his true colors. He showed me exactly who I don't want to be.

I know this is a very personal story, and I've been candid. I tell it to help you. If you find yourself relating to my experience, I pray any ill-intended words spoken to you will no longer hold you back. Be free from them. Now go do what you know in your heart to do.

We all need to erase the voices that replay in our heads from others who don't want us to be successful. Don't base your decisions on advice from people who don't have to deal with the results and who don't have your best interest at heart.

41 Jesus Didn't Say, "Follow Christians." He Said, "Follow Me."

Do you remember back in the 1990s when people wore those rubber W.W.J.D. bracelets? They were a not-so-subtle way to declare a person's faith. Athletes, celebrities, young and old, and everyday people were wearing them.

Charles Spurgeon, a well-known evangelical preacher in London, used the phrase "what would Jesus do" in quotation marks several times in a sermon he gave on June 28, 1891. He's generally credited with this thought.

Charles Sheldon reiterated it in his 1896 book *In His Steps* that was subtitled "What Would Jesus Do?"

The expression was so popular it became a snowclone, "a verbal formula that is adapted for reuse by changing only a few words so that the allusion to the original phrase remains clear" (Dictionary.com).

People began to say, "What Would Reagan Do?" and "What Would Johnny Cash Do?" Pacifists said, "Who Would Jesus Bomb?" and atheists said, "What Would Darwin Do?" Advertisers said, "What Would Jesus Buy?"

I even joined in.

Over the years I got to know a well-meaning, but somewhat controlling, Christian leader. For comfort's sake, let's call him Jonathan Lee. I used to say I was going to create a bracelet saying W.W.J.L.D.—"What Would Jonathan Lee Do?" *Every time*, and I mean dozens of times, I shared my WWJLD idea with any of his followers, they would immediately laugh, nod their head, and with a certain knowing look on their face, admit they thought about him the same way.

Yes, we are to be imitators of God. Yes, we can learn from others' victories and mistakes, insights, and experiences. Certainly, God uses others to help us and guide us. But don't fall for formulas from people who may not have your best interest in mind; "I did it this way, and you should too!"

"Be careful when you blindly follow the masses. Sometimes the "m" is silent" (Anonymous).

Have you found yourself pondering, I wonder what Pastor so-and-so would think about this, or what Sister —— would do? Instead of considering, "*What does the Bible say? What has God shown me?*"

One of my favorite sayings is "Faith is like a toothbrush. Everyone should have one and use it daily. But you shouldn't use someone else's."

There is God's will *in* our lives and God's will *for* our lives. God's will in our lives is the same for everyone. He wants every one of us to know Him, worship Him, walk in His forgiveness, and make it to heaven (and much more!).

God's will *for* our lives is different for *every single person*. God may want you to go to Nigeria and start an orphanage, someone else may not feel anything about helping with that cause, but feels led to volunteer at the downtown rescue mission, teach children in their local church, or be the best Kentucky Fried Chicken manager in history.

I believe when we open ourselves up to "WWJLD" instead of "What Would Jesus Do," we allow others to become our idols. Not everything you're hearing from others is what God is saying.

You can study, follow, and imitate others but never really know them. They differ a hundred ways from what you publicly see them to be and from who you are.

Here is the challenge for all of us: that we do not depend too much on others for our personal direction. If we do, we will feel like we've lost our way, but really, we've only let someone else borrow it.

Reclaim your brain. Think and know for yourself.

42

Be Humble; You Could Be Wrong.

"Be completely humble and gentle; be patient, bearing with one another in love" (Eph. 4:2 NIV). Humility is not thinking less of yourself. It's thinking of yourself less. Everything you do doesn't need to be seen or heard.

"Be humble, or you'll stumble" (Dwight L. Moody).

No, we don't always get what we want, but let's humbly consider this: there are people who will never have what we have right now.

"If you are humble nothing will touch you, neither praise nor disgrace, because you know what you are" (Mother Teresa).

"For everyone who exalts himself will be humbled, and he who humbles himself will be exalted" (Luke 14:11 ESV). Humble yourself, and submit to Him. "Stay true in the dark and humble in the spotlight" (Harold B. Lee).

Never look down on anyone. Only God sits up that high.

Humble yourself or life will do it for you.

Some time ago I went to a Mexican fast-food restaurant. As I stood in line for service, I noticed in front of me a very poor elderly lady who looked like a street person. I concluded that about her because she was carrying a grocery bag filled to the top with what looked like all her possessions in the world.

When it was her turn, she ordered some water and one taco. Sitting in the booth right next to her, I couldn't help but observe her and be moved with compassion for her. Shortly after I began my meal, I walked over to her and asked if I could buy some more food for her lunch.

She looked at me and angrily asked, "Who are you?"

"Just a guy who wants to help," I responded. She ignored me.

I finished my meal about the same time she did, and we both got up to leave. She began to walk out of that restaurant, and I followed her because I felt led to give her some money. In the parking lot, I approached her and offered her some cash.

Her only response was, "Stop bothering me!" Then she stormed off.

Immediately the Lord spoke this to my heart: "*That's the way My people respond to me. I'm up in heaven wanting to pour out a blessing, and they respond, 'Who are You? What do You want from me?'*" The Lord, being the gracious God that He is, continues to try to bless us. We react by saying, "*Stop bothering me.*" Missing out on the rich blessings of the Lord, we walk off, just as this lady did.

Why not humbly ask God to help you right now? He certainly wants to.

The Bible tells us that when we are weak, God makes us strong. By God's grace, be strong when you are weak. Brave when you are scared. Humble when you are victorious. "Nothing sets a person so much out of the devil's reach as humility" (Jonathan Edwards).

43 If You Let Other People Define Your World, They Will Always Make It Too Small.

About a year and a half after my first book came out, my life and ministry were exploding. God was opening amazing doors to speak, and the book was selling thousands of copies every month. I was in a season of great harvest.

I thought this would be the perfect time to go to a well-known and respected Christian leader I knew and share all that the Lord was doing and get some counsel about how to navigate what the future might hold for me. I had known him since college. The appointment was set. I was looking forward to it and had my questions all lined up.

I was about to learn a valuable lesson.

Our thirty-minute meeting began with him asking me what was happening and me sharing all the incredible things God was doing in my life—great responses when I spoke and prayed for people, substantial book sales all over the world, and more...

I ended my description by saying to him, "You have a solid and respected ministry. You know me. I thought now would be a perfect time to come to you. I'm here to open up my life to your wisdom; I want you to speak into my life."

He looked at me and began to talk. His words were not at all what I expected. The only way I know how to describe it was that he started talking to me like I was a first-year Bible school student he didn't know. The first thing out of his mouth was, "Well, don't buy a computer—I've seen too many ministers waste too much of their money there. Don't think that what's happening in your ministry now will continue to happen as it is. Do everything through your local church, and make sure you hire an ugly secretary" and a few more general, canned thoughts.

It was like I wasn't there. I don't know if he was just being careful or whether he was simply incapable of imparting into a person who was doing so much outside of his ministry. I certainly felt he did not want to take any risks in his "recommendations" to me.

Although I didn't get much out of the meeting itself, I did take away some valuable lessons I've used from that day forward. Let me share some of them with you.

When a person can no longer contribute to your life, it's time to stop going to them for direction.

Don't let it throw you if someone you respect and expect affirmation from doesn't give it to you or is unable to.

Just because a person has known you for a length of time doesn't mean they have anything to contribute to your future. Some people have no ability to see outside of their world into yours. They are an authority on one subject—themselves, and what *they* do. Maybe you can learn from them in regards to administrative details, but they can't speak into *your* life, in *your* world. So why let them?

The main point is if somebody has nothing to contribute, why talk, listen, or receive from them? As we begin to grow outside of their box, they become much more irrelevant.

Although their advice may be well-intended, they may intentionally give you nebulous, impersonal advice to decrease their risk, in case something goes wrong and makes them look bad.

Staying inside a box limits your dreams to doing the same thing over and over with the same crowd. It creates a very limited life.

You are destined for so much more than that!

44 Stagnant Waters Stink.

"He who separates himself seeks his own desire, he quarrels against all sound wisdom" (Prov. 18:1).

Separation, isolation. Don't be an island unto yourself; neither connect with people who want to control you. Controllers don't want you to connect with anyone else. They want you to know they have all the answers to all your questions, spiritually and personally.

There is no such thing as one-stop shopping for all the truth. When you're isolated, it's easier to be defeated.

We faced a question many Christian parents face. Should we send our children to a Christian or a public school? Linda and I grew up attending public schools. I think we both turned out all right—at least, I know Linda did.

We had decided to send our first two children to a local Christian school, but it was now time for our next two to start school. We had just moved back to Tulsa after a three-year stint running a publishing company in Orlando, so we were starting over in Tulsa.

The public schools where we live are excellent, known for top academics and a great, positive (mostly Christian) environment. At the same time, we knew what we were going to get at the local Christian school.

A pastor friend was at our house, Bill Scheer. Pastor Bill started a great church in Tulsa, GUTS Church. Bill encouraged us to consider the public school. He has always been about being a light where there's darkness. In my opinion, probably no other church in our city reaches the lost in as many arenas as his. I did, however, find it kind of interesting in a good way that a pastor would recommend a public school over a Christian one.

We were determined to consider both. We had experience with the Christian school—mostly good. We ventured out to the public. In fact, Linda took the lead, interviewing teachers and administrators, asking questions. Then on one of her visits, God decided to show us the way.

Inside the school, she felt strongly the Lord wanted her to drop to her knees and dedicate our children for His glory in that school. As she did, it became clear they should go to the public school. Without hesitation, we enrolled them.

Not long after, we received a letter from the superintendent of the Christian school to all parents saying it was God's will for *every* student to attend *only* a Christian school. Frankly, this letter ticked me off. I thought, *How can that possibly be true? Where would you put them all?* I also thought, *He probably attended a public school growing up*. Oh well...

Thankfully, we were secure in our faith and our relationship with the Lord, no matter what one man's opinion was. I hate it when people proclaim absolutes about something they absolutely should be open to God's will about. I dislike it because it causes people to make wrong decisions. One size does not fit all.

The letter was saying, "Don't think and don't discover for yourself." And, in so many words, keep God out of it.

By the way, our experience at the public school was good. It was the very best for our kids. Glad we listened and obeyed God.

The truth isn't hard to see; what's difficult is when people add to it.

True freedom comes from knowing for yourself.

No one person has all the answers. No one organization has all the answers and opportunities. Belief in one human authority is the greatest enemy of truth.

You've heard of the Four Spiritual Laws? The foundation premise is that "God loves you, and He has a wonderful plan for your life."

Have you found yourself feeling that another person, organization, or church believes "God loves you and *we* have a wonderful plan for your life"?

Watch out for someone or something that tries to be everything in your life. Could it be, the reason they want to separate you is not for your individual benefit, but rather because they feel threatened by others?

If you accept this, it will limit your possibilities and shrink your dream to fit within theirs. That isn't best for you or your family.

If someone says they have all the answers for everything, watch out!

It's good to have people in your life who say, "I don't know." It's bizarre for people to think they know everything.

The truth is that leaders and organizations that feel they always know what's best for you, don't always. Ironically, they are usually the least qualified to show you the way. They have lived in their own little universe; with their own language and activities. They have no capacity to interact with the great big world out there.

God loves to show Himself to you in so many ways. I've heard His voice from a billboard, song, complete silence, a pastor, a friend, and even someone I don't usually agree with.

We need a mixture of influences in our lives. "Plans fail for lack of counsel, but with many advisers they succeed" (Prov. 15:22).

45 Opportunities Are Coming to You and By You Every Day.

It was a beautiful Thursday. I had taken the afternoon off and was out playing golf with my son, Greg. As usual, he was beating me.

My cell phone rang, and I answered. It was truly a long-distance call. Peter Lowe, my friend and the founder of Success Seminars, was calling from his plane as he flew over the Atlantic Ocean from London to the U.S.

"John, I need you to speak for me next Tuesday at our event in North Carolina. I need you to take Larry King's place on the platform." I had heard that Larry King had just received emergency heart surgery. Now, because of that, I was to be his substitute!

I told Peter, "Of course I can, I'd be honored." I hung up. I played lousy the rest of the round. I knew this was the "big time." I would be speaking along with Barbara Bush, Dick Vitale, Zig Ziglar, and several other famous speakers. In fact, Peter told me I would be closing the event (as Larry King normally did), so I needed to "knock it out of the park" and leave people feeling great.

I arrived the day before the event. I wanted to make sure I was prepared and ready to go, but I didn't sleep very well. I had the same vivid dream, over and over again. In the dream I was standing behind the stage, hearing an announcement that Larry King would not be here tonight, but instead, we would have...*John Mason!*

As I dreamed, I saw thirteen thousand people streaming out of the arena as I tried to give a speech to a moving target.

Of course, nothing like that happened. Peter did a great job introducing me. The speech went well, and the crowd was great. I got to meet a lot of famous people backstage. An hour with Dick Vitale was unforgettable. And now I get to tell you this story.

Remember, what you fear rarely happens. You lose when you let fear keep you from doing what you thought you were afraid to do. Although I could have viewed this invitation and the timing of it as too intimidating to do, I didn't. I kept in mind that it was a great opportunity, and I knew God wanted me to do it.

Excuses will always be there for you. Opportunities won't. "Don't spend so much time trying to choose the perfect opportunity that you miss the right opportunity" (Michael Dell).

Our walk with God begins with the word "follow" and ends with the word "go!" The devil hates when he hears a believer say, "I'll do what you tell me to do, Lord." Go ahead. You never know what goodness will be on the other side of your action.

Opportunities are impatient and may not wait for you, so try to be ready for the opportunity before the opportunity is there. Opportunity dances with those already on the dance floor.

Availability is the greatest ability you have. There is always time and opportunity. Don't be lost out in the backyard looking for four-leaf clovers when opportunity knocks at your front door.

Be ready. Say yes!

Your opportunity is here.

46 Seize the Way.

It was a brilliant day...and I was panicking.

Having just left church, I wandered from the dark air-conditioned auditorium into the bright noonday sun. My eyes scanned the vast parking lot of several thousand cars for my own, but it was nowhere to be found. My old Chevrolet Caprice Classic—broken front seat and all—had been stolen...at church!

Strangely, I had an epiphany! My thoughts flowed from fear to fortune as I thought, *Maybe it's really gone and I can get some much-needed cash for that old clunker.*

With each passing moment, I felt happier and happier with my newfound "miracle," until I unexpectedly and disappointingly found it—parked right where I had left it, hidden between two Oklahoma-sized pickup trucks.

What was I actually looking for? A car? Not really. I was looking for change. You might say, I was looking for change in all the wrong places. So many of us do that.

We want others to change, circumstances to change, our location or job to change. Rather, now is the time for *you and I* to fully embrace the person God created us to be.

"Change. It can be hard. It requires no extra effort to settle for the same old thing. Auto-pilot keeps us locked into past patterns. But transforming your life? That requires courage, commitment, and effort. It's tempting to stay camped in the land of That's-Just-How-It-Is. But to get to the good stuff in life, you must be willing to become an explorer and adventurer" (John Mark Green).

Making a life-change is pretty scary. But you know what's even scarier? Regret.

As you make your change, don't be afraid of what could go wrong; instead, focus your thoughts on what could go right. Change is not a painful ending—it's a new beginning. You're about to meet the real you!

Playing it safe is probably the most unsafe thing in the world. You cannot stand still. You must go forward and be open to those adjustments that improve you.

Focus your energy, not on recapturing the old, but on building the new. Stop looking for happiness in the same place you lost it.

Nothing changes if nothing changes. Close some doors. They no longer go where you're supposed to be.

The changes I'm presenting in this book can be uncomfortable. But, great things never come from the comfort zone. Never assume that you're stuck with the way things are right now. You aren't. Don't settle for an unhappy life. Life changes every single moment, and so can you.

A Final Word

"May you believe—with all your heart—that God is writing a great story with your life! May the lies that came your way today fall by the wayside and not make their way into your heart. May you instead know and believe the truth about who you are and whose you are. You are loved, accepted, gifted, and treasured. You have important things to do in this life. May you refuse to let anything distract you from God's highest and best purposes for you. He'll make a way where there seems to be no way. He'll move mountains at just the right time. You can trust Him. So, trust Him" (Susie Larson).

Live authentically,
Grow continuously,
Celebrate people,
Hope for the best,
Serve others,
Give your all,
Be free,
Walk humbly,
Love God, love others.

AUTHOR CONTACT

John Mason welcomes the opportunity to speak at churches, conferences, and various business settings. For more information, to schedule John Mason to speak, or for author coaching and publishing services, please contact:

John Mason
Insight International
contact@freshword.com
www.freshword.com
(918) 493-1718

If you have any prayer needs, please don't hesitate to contact us.

AUTHOR PRODUCTS

Additional copies of *Genuine Imitation* are available from your local or online bookstore, in e-book format, or directly from:

John Mason
Insight International
contact@freshword.com
www.freshword.com
(918) 493-1718

Also available are the following books, audio, and author writing resources:

Books:
An Enemy Called Average
Be Yourself
Believe You Can
Conquering an Enemy Called Average
Dare to Be
Fall Seven Times—Stand Up Eight
Know Your Limits—Then Ignore Them
Let Go of Whatever Makes You Stop
Proverbs Prayers
You Can Do It
You're Born an Original—Don't Die a Copy

Audio:
Nuggets of Success CD series
This series includes ten CDs of best-selling titles:
An Enemy Called Average
You're Born an Original—Don't Die a Copy!
Let Go of Whatever Makes You Stop
Conquering an Enemy Called Average

The Ultimate Author Tool:

John Mason has created an all-inclusive, A-to-Z guide to write the book of your dreams and sell it everywhere you can! The 164-page manual covers what you need to know about the writing, publishing, and selling of your book. Also included are three CDs and three DVDs with nearly seven hours of combined teaching from John Mason himself.

ABOUT THE AUTHOR

John Mason is an internationally recognized best-selling author, speaker, minister, and author coach. He's the founder and president of Insight International and Insight Publishing Group, organizations dedicated to helping people reach their dreams and fulfill their God-given destiny.

He has authored twenty books including *An Enemy Called Average*, *You're Born an Original—Don't Die a Copy*, *Let Go of Whatever Makes You Stop*, and *Know Your Limits—Then Ignore Them* which have sold nearly two million copies and are translated into more than thirty languages throughout the world. His books are widely known as a source of godly wisdom, scriptural motivation, and practical principles. His writings have been published in *Reader's Digest,* along with numerous other national publications, and seven of his books have reached the #1 spot on an Amazon best-seller list.

Known for his quick wit, powerful thoughts, and insightful ideas, he is a popular speaker across the U.S. and around the world.

John and his wife, Linda, have four children: Michelle, Greg, Michael, and David. They reside in Tulsa, Oklahoma.

Off the Couch, Back to Business!

Other titles in the Keys4Business series:

The Universal Guide To Business Networking
Terry Bean

The Twitter Workbook
David R. Haslam

The Marketing Playbook
Debbie Scartozzi

The Customer's Way
Daniel H. Walker

Off the Couch, Back to Business!

April Scarlett

Plymouth, MI, U.S.A.
www.PublishHMSI.com

Off the Couch, Back to Business!

Published by HMSI Publishing L.L.C., a division of HMSI, inc.
www.PublishHMSI.com

by April Scarlett
www.aprilscarlett.com

Copy Editing by Geoffrey Bankowski
Proofreading by Lynn Gregory

Cover Design by Stephanie L. Wilkins

Book Design Completed in Plymouth, U.S.A.

Publishing Coordination by Jessica A. Paredes
Published by David R. Haslam

Permissions,
HMSI Publishing L.L.C.
Suite 3b,
50768 Van Buren Drive,
Plymouth, MI 48170, U.S.A.

Info@PublishHMSI.com
1.734.259.0387

ISBN – 13: 978-0-9826945-7-2

0081-0001

Printed in the United States of America

TKR 10 9 8 7 6 5 4 3 2 1
MK 31527-23898
40639 11:55 PT

For the gentlemen in my house,

James, Stone and Sam,

who inspire me every day to reach

for my ‘next great thing’.

April’s Upwords #49

The wildest dream IS possible. Don’t be afraid to hold on tight and get it

Table of Contents

How to Use This Book

This book is yours, not mine. It is a place for you to take a breath, adjust your focus and take charge of your "next great thing." I encourage you to share your thoughts, feelings and ambitions within its pages, as I will share mine. The idea is to help you with your success, through my own experiences.

The first chapter of the book, "Making a Decision for Change" is a bit of background as to what past decisions have led to where I am at this stage of my career and success. It is followed by eleven steps to help guide you to do the same, everything from how to recover from loss to what you will do with your new found success! Each step is broken down into eight sub-sections: My experience, Stats & Stuff You Need to Know, Why This Step Is So Important, Action Steps TODAY, Practical Advice, Feed Your Energy, Spin It- Turning Negative to Positive, and Summary. There is a glossary and resource section in the back. I also provided exercises and workspace to help you track your progress. Use the worksheets and write in the margins. Let this book become your handy resource and a journal of sorts. Consider me your business assistant ready to help you in any way I can.

I may have authored this book but it will be you––the reader––who will finish it. I hope you will dig in, apply the steps and really make it your own. These pages are your safe haven to recover, dream, plan and take action. Good luck in your journey, I will be right there with you along the way!

Introduction: The Cat in the Bag

Sometimes you must experience a low point in your life in order to find the motivation to set yourself back on track. For me it was the day I had to buy a bigger purse. I call it my purse moment. It's ironic, you would think a bigger purse would be needed to hold a bigger wallet, not be the red flag indicating my world was spinning out of control.

We had just gotten our car back from being repossessed. It took a mint to get it out of the lock-up, and cost double that in humiliation. I couldn't believe it when the white pick-up truck that had seemed to follow us home pulled into our driveway. A man in a ball cap pounded on my back porch door and said, "You've got five minutes to get what you want out of your car and hand me the key." I was in a panic, mostly because I was afraid five minutes wasn't going to be long enough to get all of our stuff out of the car. We had sports equipment and kid's toys and CD's and phone chargers...and the garage door opener, don't forget the garage door opener! How had this happened? Since the business was failing I had only been making partial payments, thinking something was better than nothing. I thought wrong. At least the neighbors weren't home. At least this guy and his truck hadn't shown up in town or at my son's school parking lot when I was picking him up in the afternoon. Thank goodness the kids were in school. I just stood there stunned as the repo-man hooked my car up to his truck and drove away.

We got the car back, however, the credit union representative called to let me know "Sometimes the paperwork can take awhile to get straight. If for some reason it (my car) gets picked up again, you'll be able to get it out if you show your copy." What? Picked up again! Because of a paperwork glitch? I thought about how often I would be looking over my shoulder for that white pick-up truck and guy in the ball cap. The fear of going through the entire ordeal again was upsetting enough, but what brought me to a near panic attack was something else.

At the time, my youngest son carried around his stuffed toy cat named Milky. We all treated this darn thing like a member of the family. She got tucked in at night, "fed" in the morning and taken to the doctor with my son. He took her everywhere except to school. Milky was ragged and worn, with a body smushed flat, but she was his best friend. She was and still is priceless and irreplaceable. When it came to school, my son would bring her in the car, hug her goodbye and go about his day. He always dealt with it fine as long as she was still next to his seat in the back to greet him upon his return after school.

Suddenly, due to this unfortunate prolonged threat of the repo man, the car was no longer a safe place for Milky to lay in wait for her human to get out of school. I used to think nothing of leaving her in the car while I grocery shopped or ran other errands. Even if I was at home, I'd often leave her in the backseat so she'd be sure to be there for the afternoon bell. But this was no longer the case. There was no way I could risk the car being taken with Milky in it. Just the thought of having to explain to my son why his toy cat was gone brought me to tears. There was only one thing to do, for now, until this whole car thing was straightened out. I'd get a bigger purse to fit Milky in so I could keep her secure… just in case. It would be different if I went home every day while the kids were in school, but around this time it was rare that that happened. What was I supposed to do with her? We hadn't told our boys anything yet…not about losing the business, the car or the house. I didn't want to explain why he should leave the cat home. Surely it would upset his routine at school. I just wanted to keep everyone happy until we had to start packing. I would just keep the cat in my bag.

Some who read this might think I'm crazy, with the exception of the parents who know exactly what I'm talking about. Their kids have special stuffies too. The trauma of a lost "best friend" at such a young age is a major deal, and we parents go to great lengths to secure them.

Every time I needed something from my purse I would see Milky, and I would be more determined than ever to get us out of this mess. That determination fueled my thoughts for change, which turned into actions. Actions led to where I am today. Step by step I climbed up and away from having a cat in my bag. Whatever your setback, whatever your "cat in the bag", let this book be a guide to helping you find your own correct path.

April's Upwords #33

There is a reason we jump up to the next step, instead of down, when the step we are on begins to crumble. It is our instinct to move forward.

Step One: Mindset

My Experience

I hadn't been off my couch in three weeks. It was the first week in February, and I wondered how I would celebrate my upcoming 38th birthday, on what should have been the first anniversary of my storybook-themed play café named Beanstalks. I didn't want to answer the phone, look at my email inbox or attend meetings. I had failed, and everybody knew it. How could I face my colleagues and fellow board members? What was I supposed to say at community meetings? And what about the naysayers who thought me a fool for leaving the phone company in the first place to open my own business? How many "I told you so's" would I have to endure? I was saddened by my loss, and ashamed to show my face.

It wasn't like I didn't have any business to tend to. Beanstalks was full of assets that needed to be dispersed. I owed everybody money and wasn't sure how to deal with any of them. Bill collectors called from Washington, Michigan, Pennsylvania and New York for equipment leases. Locally, I was behind on rent, and had defaulted on bank loans.

Then there was my family, whom I felt I let down the most. My six year old son was in tears every day after school, wanting to play at what had become his home away from home, and couldn't understand why we were locked out of "our" Beanstalks. My teenager was missing his job there, and my husband had spent the last three weeks clearing out all of our personal belongings from the space, while trying his best to keep me from crumbling. Not once did he blame me, but I blamed myself enough for the both of us.

There did come a time however, after weeks of doing nothing, that I realized I had to make a change. It was not unlike the stirrings I had had at the phone company. Somewhere deep inside I had a voice who reminded me that my life was meant to be more than this, that it was time to buck up and take responsibility so I could move on to whatever was next. I knew there was something else. I knew my experience from Beanstalks would take me there.

In the spaces below, and in several areas throughout the book, there is room to write things down specific to your situation. Writing out your thoughts is a great way to clarify your ideas and give you something tangible to refer back to. It is also a way to take action, and every action leads to another and another. Think of these exercises as a way to keep your momentum moving forward.

Fill in the spaces to help you transition from one step to the next:

The toughest part so far has been______________

____

____

____

I will feel better about this tough time if I_______

____

____

____

I am most proud of___________________________

____

____

____

Stats and Stuff You Need to Know

According to SCORE Counselors to America's Small Business, seven out of ten businesses make it to at least their second year, and only half survive to five years. In 2008, the year of Beanstalks, there were 627,200 new businesses in the United States, and 595,600 businesses closed. A business closure is not necessarily a failure, as some who use their exit strategies gracefully will call themselves a success. A failure, however, occurs when the outcome overwhelms stability.

I would like to re-emphasize what a valuable resource SCORE can be. This is a huge group of retired business professionals who give their time just to counsel newbies, business owners, and entrepreneurs like you and me. Did I mention the services offered by SCORE are free? This is an organization that was very helpful in the research aspect of Beanstalks before I opened, and was especially helpful and compassionate when I knew I was losing the business. As a matter of fact, once we discussed and realized I would be forced into bankruptcy, it was my SCORE rep that found my excellent attorney, who specialized in business bankruptcy.

The loss of a business is considered a major trauma, not unlike a divorce, especially if the result of the loss affects the living arrangements and financial stability of your household. Some studies indicate financial stress as the number one cause for divorce. Overwhelming financial instability may also lead to depression and a number of physical ailments. A study conducted in 2005 looked at over six thousand people struggling with high levels of debt. Each of them, at some point over the duration of their financial stress, reported failing physical health.

Negative Health Effects of Financial Stress

by O'Neill, Sorhaindo, Jing and Garman

Consumer Interests Annual Vol. 51 2005

www.personalfinancefoundation.org

Health Effects of Financial Problems	**Frequency (Pecentage)**
Stress/stressed out	613 (46.3%)
Worry, nerves, tension, anxiety, pressure	157 (11.9%)
Depression/depressed	132 (10.0%)
Insomnia and sleep disorders /problems	122 (9.2%)
Headaches/migraines	96 (7.3%)
High blood pressure/hypertension	95 (7.2%)
Stomach/abdominal/digestive problems	38 (2.9%)
Other aches and pains (e.g. back,chest)	16 (1.2%)
Ulcers or possible ulcers	13 (1.0%)
Appetite disorders and weight gain or loss	46 (3.5%)
Fatigue and feeling tired/weak	14 (1.1%)
Drug, alcohol, or cigarette use	4 (.3%)
General or other sicknesses	85 (6.4%)
Unable to afford or access health care services and exams	8 (.6%)
Can't afford/don't follow recommended health maintenance practices	22 (1.7%)
Other responses	111 (8.4%)

I don't elaborate on these kinds of statistics as a scare tactic. It's just that stress is serious business and can be very harmful to your health. Thus the reason I encourage you to avoid it when you can, and deal with it when you cannot.

If you are an entrepreneur like I am, and can muster up the spirit and energy to just keep going, you can turn the loss and the stress into gain and exuberance. I love what author and speaker John C. Maxwell says about failure, "failure is simply a price we pay to achieve success, and if we learn to embrace that new definition of failure, then we can move ahead."

Why This Step (Mindset) Is So Important

"It's time to start living the life you imagined." This phrase is engraved on a rock that I keep on my desk. My son Stone and I were shopping one day at a cool bookstore in downtown Ann Arbor, not really looking for anything in particular. They had all kinds of rocks and plaques with different quotes, but nothing I was dying to take home. Then my son caught my attention from the front of the store. "This is the one mom," he said. He had found the rock with the quote and he was right. I think the best part of the story is the fact that he knows me so well, and knows my message, that he was able to put his finger on just the right one. We are both inspired by this rock and now I take it around to all of my publicity and promotional events. It is the essence of what I do and who I am. I know if I stop imagining what will be, what I expect of my future, then my dreams will never happen, and that is completely and utterly unacceptable.

"Thoughts become things" is another phrase I live by. I've read it, watched it, heard it and observed it. It is, in one form or another, in every self-help book and any spirit-boosting infomercial or talk show. It is the idea that what we create in our mind becomes our reality. I describe it as "positive knowing." It is not the same as wishful thinking, or any form of magic. It is seeing something for yourself so vividly and with such emotion, that subconsciously you begin to take the steps you need to get there, so that the thought is now your existence. I know, I know, we are back to the naysayers who don't believe anyone can do anything, who think this is a bit of hocus pocus. Don't listen to those people, and get that doubt out of your very capable brain! I know this idea works because I have used it on more than one occasion (which I will talk about later in the book). I also know that self-doubt will stop it in its tracks. Set your mind. See a successful future. If you don't believe you can make something of yourself, then how are you supposed to accomplish anything? It is about making a choice. Are you going to let your setback beat you?

Take Action TODAY

(about 20 minutes each)

1. Decide to move forward. Write this down, hang it where you can see it, and repeat it every day, out loud, especially upon waking or before going to sleep.

"Today I make the choice to move forward. I learn from past mistakes and have set my mind toward a successful future. I am smart, capable and reach any goal I set for myself from this day on."

2. Find a way to relax. Anxiety is an open door to mental and physical ailments. My choice is exercise. You don't need to do an aerobic boot camp or kickboxing marathon, a simple walk will do. Exercise releases endorphins (the feel good hormones). If you don't want to exercise, then learn deep breathing, watch a funny movie or soak in a bubbly tub. Whatever it takes to give you a little bit of me-time each day, even twenty minutes will do the trick.

These are my three favorite ways to relax*: (circle the days you will do each. Mix it up so you don't get bored)*

1. ____

M T W Th F Sa Su

2.____

M T W Th F Sa Su

3.____

M T W Th F Sa Su

Practical Advice

It's time to climb out from underneath the piles and piles of unfinished business. We'll get into specifics in a later chapter, but for now you need to get organized. Make different piles or lists for financials, taxes, employees, customers, assets, services, people to contact to let know you are out of business, and people to thank. You can't fix a problem if you can't see it. Once you have it all in front of you, you will see a path to get through it. The sooner you deal, the sooner you move on.

Feed Your Energy

You are absolutely justified in feeling the loss of what you created. The thing about human nature, when it comes to failure, no matter how shrewd we are as businesswomen / men, how competitive in the boardroom or authoritative at the helm of our own businesses, when we fail, we are taken down emotionally as much as we are professionally. It breaks our hearts whether we are nurturing a child, a marriage or a sales contract. When something happens to what we have created, we take it personally.

Sit on the couch, eat the chocolate, and channel surf, just be sure and not do it for too long. For me, it was three weeks, and that was probably too much. The most challenging obstacle was forgiving myself. Once I was able to do that, I could find reasons to be grateful, and I always say "it is impossible to feel down when you are being grateful." Thank your lucky stars for something, and your mood will begin to spiral back up. If it doesn't, then find someone who can help get you to a starting point. It is so surprising to me there is still a stigma attached to getting professional help for our mental health. I cannot fully express how talk therapy has aided my recovery. There is no shame in seeking help so get it, feel better, and get on with your future picture!

Spin It: Turning Negative to Positive

Obstacles for me during this time of immediate reaction were clear. My biggest fear was wondering what other people would think of me. How could I show my face? One of my landlords, of all people, said to me, "Well April, you did something really great here. You took an idea and turned it into something real. There aren't a lot of people who do that. You're going to be just fine." The truth was, I did do something really great. Beanstalks was a beautiful, enchanting place, complete with laughing children and chatty parents, good coffee and fantastic cookies (thanks Robin!). It was exactly as I had pictured it in my head. It was respectable, allergy free and clean, clean, clean! That is really something to brag about in the indoor playground business. There were a lot of great things that came out of Beanstalks, and I made the decision to be proud instead of ashamed.

Step One: Mindset Summary

- Remember my story, I never thought I would get off that couch, but I did!
- You are not alone, businesses fail.
- Attitude is everything, remind yourself how capable you are, be confident .
- Get a grip on emotions, anxiety is bad, and relaxation is good. Find a healthy way to feel good, even if it means seeking professional help…its okay!
- Take stock of what you need to handle--make a list or create “piles” so you know how far you have to go to be free of it.
- Forgive yourself.
- Negative to positive, identify your obstacles and re-think them.

April's Upwords #3

Say nice things to yourself. You are always listening, whether you realize it or not.

Step Two: Due Credit

Note: Steps two and three will coincide with steps four and beyond. They are reminders that you must take care of yourself and your psyche while you go through the process of rebuilding your future. Goals are more easily reached when you are feeling well and confident.

My Experience

Despite the heartbreak of losing my business, there are little gems that still present themselves to reinforce the notion that Beanstalks was a worthwhile endeavor. I still have children come up to me in my son's school and tell me how much they miss it. I still have customers who became friends, who I meet up with for coffee, because they missed hanging out and chatting over a latte (a Fair Trade, Ethiopian blend latte!). I still have thank you cards and photos from parents and children who swear their child's birthday party, which I created, was their most magical to date, and how I and my business will forever be a part of their child's memories. I met children's authors who shared their publishing tips. I hired great people, some of whom are still a part of my life today.

One of my favorite accomplishments is the environment I created for my customers. I took an old, beautiful building with bones of the church it had become nearly 100 years ago, and turned it into an enchanting, story book castle. There were banners hung around the perimeter of the high ceiling. Rapunzel and her long locks of hair towered above guests as they would enter. Gold gilded picture frames surrounding posters of nursery rhymes like Peas Porridge Hot and Jack Be Nimble hung throughout the Beanstalks castle. A spiral staircase led to my tower upstairs, my office, a fairy tale perch of my own. There were books abound, as reading and storybooks were a huge part of our business. Little chairs and comfy furniture lent themselves to story times and individual reading. There was our three tiered indoor climber with spiral slide, which delighted our youngest visitors and at times challenged their courage. There was nothing better to hear than a squealing "I did it!" from atop the highest point, from a young child who had finally climbed all the way to the top.

Equally as important is the catapult the business gave me into my community. Without my title as a business owner, I would have never joined the groups and organizations that are such an integral part of what my city is all about. These were groups like the Downtown Merchants Association or the local chapter of the Chamber of Commerce. I would have never made presentations in front of City Council, or have taken a definitive place on the list of people to call when volunteers are needed for something taking place within our community.

When the idea of Beanstalks first popped into my head, I didn't even know what a business plan was, or that I even needed one! I had to take the time to learn many skills otherwise foreign to me. I had to research customer demographics, profit and loss, how to schedule contractors and manage construction. I learned about plumbing, planning, and a ton about food and safety requirements! I know what fire safety entails for places of business, insurance that is needed and I gained clarity about taxes. I learned copyright law when it comes to naming your business and how advertising can either help or hurt you. I took lessons from mentors and advice from customers. Every day was something else for me to add to my repertoire of skills. The business may be gone, but the things I learned (some of them the hard way!) while it was up and running, are priceless assets to me today.

Bottom line, like the child atop the climber, "I did it!" I built a business from scratch and learned from it. I know what went right and what I did wrong and like every other entrepreneur, I have taken what I learned and journeyed on to what is next. For me, I couldn't possibly be doing what I am today or be the person I have become without Beanstalks. What I thought was sure to be a destination place for my career, turned out to be a necessary stepping stone that I would need for my bigger picture.

Stats and Stuff You Need To Know

There is something to be said for learning as you go. As said by Confucius, "I hear and I forget; I see and I remember; I do and I understand." A degree in Business or Entrepreneurial Studies certainly puts you a step-ahead when it comes to certain aspects of creating a business. However, don't feel like you cannot become a business owner without one, or while you are pursuing your education. For me, the entire process of opening, maintaining (even if only for a short time), and losing a business was a wealth of information and education. Learning by doing, or Action Learning, is actually the preferred form of obtaining knowledge in many countries in Europe, Australia and other parts of the world.

It is an educational process where people study their own actions and experiences in order to improve performance. It is similar to teaching through examples and repetitions, and has its own formula for success.

Action Learning was created by a professor Reginald Revans. He developed the method in the United Kingdom in the 1940s after observing workers and managers of a specific industry. He encouraged managers to get together and discuss problems or experiences they were having, and then to seek solutions or problem solving suggestions from each other. The approach resulted in escalated productivity and Revans knew he was onto something. I love what he said, "People had to be aware of their lack of relevant knowledge and be prepared to explore the area of their ignorance with suitable questions and help from other people in similar positions." The Action Learning Formula is:

L (Learning) = P (Programmed Knowledge) + Q (Questions).

In other words, you learn best when you combine your book smarts with experiences from, and a curiosity about, others in the same position as yourself. I wish I had known more about this formula when I opened Beanstalks. Perhaps I would have sought fellow business owners' perspectives sooner. Again, a good way to do this is to seek out business associations near you or even professional chat rooms, where ideas and problem solving can take place in a comfortable environment. Also, there are many websites and brick and mortar firms who specialize in Action Learning, so don't hesitate to do a quick search on the web to see if one of these companies is for you.

Why This Step (Due Credit) Is So Important

Everything you have achieved in your life, including in business, is a lesson. You have to give yourself credit for what you have accomplished if you want to keep moving your future forward. You know the things you did right, most likely because they were in areas of your expertise and came easily. Acknowledge the fact that you knew those things and succeeded with them. You also know what you didn't do right. These tend to stick in our minds more because they hang over our heads in big, block letters that read "IF ONLY I HAD...(done something different, knew more, asked sooner), THEN PERHAPS I'D STILL BE IN BUSINESS." Regret will hurt you. It will rob you of your creativity, banish your courage and keep you stuck in nowhere -ville. Give yourself credit, take what you've learned, suck up what's left, and get on with your future!

Take Action TODAY

(about 20-60 minutes each)

1. Explore different learning processes to find what fits you best. Do some research on Active Learning or check out recommended business reading lists, like the one available from *Business Weekly*.
2. See what business networking groups are available where you are setting up shop. Look for Merchant Organizations, Chambers of Commerce and networking groups. There are some out there specifically for women, find these types of lists on the National Organization for Women website, one of my favorites.

These are the local business networking groups in my area:

Organization	Web Address	Phone
Chmber of Commerce		
Merchants Association		

3. Take note of a time when you felt appreciated in your business. Write it down and keep it where you can see it, to remind you of how worthy you were of that appreciation. If you are really moved, write a quick note to the person who made you feel that way and thank them. This will force you to remember an accomplishment... so give yourself credit!

Use this space to note a time when you really felt appreciated in your business:

(Who?)____from

____really

made me feel appreciated when he/she _______________

____

____

____

____

I will thank them by________________________________

____

Practical Advice

It is time to update your resume. Make a list of all of the new skills you gained in your business. Take credit for these things, and work them into your resume. Here is what my list looked like after Beanstalks closed. Remember, even if you learned the hard way that resulted in a failure, you must acknowledge the fact that you now know what *not to do* the next time. This still counts as a skill.

Skills Gained through Beanstalks

1. How to write a business plan
2. How to pitch an idea
3. How to take credit cards
4. Experts I need on my team
5. Health and food safety
6. How to hire employees/ taxes
7. How to handle copyright
8. How to hire contractors/freelancers
9. Which alarm systems are right for your business
10. It is better to stage progress than to try and achieve it all at once
11. Community involvement
12. Effective/ineffective advertising
13. What a mentor can do
14. The ins and outs of bankruptcy
15. Spending discipline
16. Stellar customer service
17. The art of a coffee bar
18. Interior design (as was appropriate for my space)

There is more and more I add to this list as I move forward. Every action I took with Beanstalks caused a positive or negative result, both of which add to my knowledge base, and your list will do the same for you!

Use this space to list all of the skills you have gained through your business experience. Don't be shy! Think about business and social skills.

Feed Your Energy

One of the best ways to feed your energy is to give back to others, this ties right in with giving yourself credit, or exercising self-acknowledgment. If you know you have accomplished something, you can share it. Take something you learned from your past experience as a business person and share it with someone else who is seeking it. Don't be surprised if others who are trying to start your same kind of business call you for advice. It may sting at first, and nobody is asking for your secrets, but you probably have solid advice to give. I made the mistake of being offended when I received a call (immediately after I had closed the business) from a couple trying to open their own play café, and never could muster up the courage to talk to them. This plagued me for awhile, and all of the negative feelings about not helping them certainly didn't help me get off the couch! I eventually learned to give back in other ways by reaching out and volunteering within my community. Toast yourself for your accomplishments and then find a way to give the gift of your experience to someone who needs it!

Spin It: Turning Negative to Positive

Obstacles for me in this step were the pity parties and the whispers about my having lost the business. In truth, there probably weren't as many as I thought, but I do know people who couldn't believe I had taken such a risk when I had "obviously" not known what I was doing, who thought I was "scattered" and should retreat. There are still people today who don't take me seriously, even as a writer, because the "real" business I had is no more.

If there are people in your life who are sending this negativity your way, I have good news for you. Only you can make yourself feel bad. No one else can do that to you unless you let them. Be empowered. Take care of you and your business and your future success. Those people will come around, and if they do not, you choose to not be around them, or if that is impossible, you choose to be unaffected by them. Like April's Upwords #12, "Surround yourself with people who lift you up, to keep you just out of reach from anyone wanting to bring you down."

Step Two: Due Credit Summary

- Remember my story, really focus on the good things you did, what you learned and your achievements.
- Find the best method of learning that works for you.
- Self-acknowledgement is a necessary step to moving forward with confidence.
- Start your how-to-business reading list, thank someone who appreciated you.
- List all skills gained from your experience and get them fitted into your resume.
- Find a way to give back!
- Surround yourself with people who support and energize you, don't be dragged down.

April's Upwords #28

Breathe people. In through your nose, out through your mouth. Your brain is amazing and powerful; feed it some oxygen so you can make the most of it!

Step Three: Self Care

My Experience

When Beanstalks began to struggle, I began to struggle. I didn't sleep. I stopped eating. If I did eat, it was a quick chocolate muffin to go with my gallons per day of coffee. I worried constantly. I guess you could say I was in a constant state of anxiety and near panic. I saw my place slipping away from me, and instead of seeking positive reinforcements, I buried myself in self-doubt and fear. I should not have been surprised then, the day my body said, "No more!"

It was about fifteen minutes before I was scheduled to open. I was alone, as my day shift employee hadn't yet arrived. I bent down to open a box of paper coffee cups and restock the shelf. The pain hit my lower back so sharply, so instantaneously, and with such gusto that I fell back onto the floor. To this day, I don't know how I managed to pull myself back up, gripping the cabinets until I was at least leaning on the counter. At that time, our local Chamber Director stopped in for a visit. He could see I couldn't move, and was in a lot of pain. It's a good thing he stopped by because I wound up asking him to pull my car up to the door (literally, on the sidewalk to the door) and drive me to the chiropractor (Dr. P. a lifesaver!). I had NEVER felt this much pain. I remember sitting in the passenger seat of my own car in tears, thinking "I can't believe I am crying in front of Larry!"

This is what can happen. Fatigue + poor nutrition + constant worry = disaster. Your body knows when you are overdoing it. The key is to keep yourself from getting to that point. I definitely learned the hard way. That injury kept me in my recliner for more than three weeks.

Stats and Stuff You Need to Know

Everyone has a weak spot, whether you suffer from migraines, have arthritis or live with something more chronic like allergies, asthma or worse. When you let your defenses down, your immunity, you are more likely to get hit where you are weak. For me it was my lower back and my asthma.

Of course you will check with your doctor and not rely on me to make choices for your health, but here is some basic information that I like to brush up on, especially when I'm not feeling my best.

When it comes to fatigue, it is simple; you've got to sleep. I am a serious night owl. I get most ambitious, most creative and driven, sometimes beginning at 9:30PM. I think it probably comes from working from home, and being most productive after my kids have gone to sleep, and I've had some one on one time with my husband. The problem with this is it leaves me wanting to work until 2am, and I still have the alarm going off to get the kids ready for school at 6:30 am. But, because I know how important sleep is, I still find ways to fit it in, even if I simply set the alarm on my phone for a quick twenty minutes before I pick the kids up from school. Actually, after doing some research it appears I'm onto something. According to Mark Stibich, Ph. D, napping protects your health and makes you more productive. He reports a study of 24,000 Greek individuals who napped several times a week had lower risks of dying from heart disease. And, people who nap at work have lower levels of stress, improved memory, cognitive function and mood. Also, the CARDIA sleep study, as reported in the Journal of the American Medical Association, concludes a definitive link between less sleep and hypertension. Bottom line, adequate sleep is necessary for optimal health.

Nutrition is the second part of the equation when it comes to feeling your best. The most common recommendations are to eliminate caffeine and alcohol. I fall short here because anybody who knows me knows I'm a java queen. Next, eat small meals/snacks every three to four hours with some protein, even if it's just a handful of mixed nuts. Load up on fruits and veggies, drink at least three 8 oz. glasses of water (I like sparkling water), cut down on junk, you know the drill. Again it comes down to making a choice. Do you want to feel your best to reach your ultimate goals of success, or do you want a Twinkie for breakfast?

The last part of the equation we've already talked about back in Step One, the importance of reducing stress through exercise and relaxation. It is so important that I don't mind reiterating it here. Do something good for yourself, have a little fun, get your mind off of work once in awhile and tell yourself how awesome you are!

Why Step Three (Self Care) Is So Important

For me it is easy because I fall back on the "mom factor." If I'm not in optimal form, who is going to take care of all of the things I take care of on a daily basis for my kids and my hubby? True, my husband does a great job if I'm down, but ultimately I feel the need to take care of them. Caring for them makes me happy.

I'm the first to admit I've had cookies and coffee for breakfast, but if I can remember to ask myself one single question before hitting the cookie jar, 100% of the time I re-route my reach to the whole grain cereal instead. The question I ask myself is, "How bad do you want IT, April?" The IT here is not the cookies, but my dream, my future, the way it plays out like a movie in my brain. If I am going to do all of the things I have planned, and open all of the doors for opportunity, I have to make good choices.

Take Action TODAY

(20 minutes each)

1. Continue exercise and relaxation techniques from Step One
2. If you haven't had an annual physical for awhile, call your doctor and schedule one (if you don't have a doctor or are without insurance, check with your local hospital or County Health and Human Services to get a list of free screenings and exams in your area (you are not alone and there are a ton of resources available, no excuses)

Date of Laast physical	New Appointment Date / Time	Dr. Contact Number

3. Set up a food journal and sleep schedule. Write down everything you put in your mouth. You'll be surprised how many times a day you sabotage your nutrition. Once you start keeping track, you'll stop and think before reaching for the bag of chips.

Example of a Food Journal Entry

Day of the week: Su M Tu W Th F Sa

Breakfast: oatmeal with raisins & cinn., wheat toast (1) with and black coffee

Lunch: one bowl minestrone soup, 2 pieces garlic bread and a cola

Dinner: steak with steak sauce, baked potato/butter/sc, green beans, merlot, pie

Snacks: chocolate covered pretzels, apple

Glasses of water: 1 2 3 4 5 6 7 8 *(circle number)*

Servings of alcohol: 1 2 3 4 5 6 7 8 *(circle number)*

Practical Advice

With your new found energy and health, you'll be more productive. Make sure you have a good weekly planner, either an app for your phone or my favorite, the old leather bound planner with tabs, pockets and to-do lists. I also urge you to sign up for emailing lists for great daily inbox reminders to take care of you. Two of my faves are *Real Age* by Dr. Oz and *Hungry Girl.*

Feed Your Energy

Go have fun. I was standing outside my son's school this week listening to two moms set up a play date for their daughters. I asked one of them, "Why don't moms have play dates?" One replied, "I can't think of the last time I had time." It's true, we are so busy building our empires and taking care of our families or pets or mowing the lawn that we put a girl's night out at the bottom of our priority list. I'm guilty too. One of my best friends and I can never seem to get our schedules lined up to meet for coffee or a cocktail, because we have countless other priorities. We always say we'll meet up once a month, a *month*, and end up seeing each other only a few times per year.

Find time for fun. Go for manicures and lunch, do dinner and a movie with your spouse/partner/current love of your life, picnic and play with your kids. Whatever it is that makes you laugh and enjoy yourself, that is what you need to do. Then, whatever you do, don't go into a guilt-fest. Time off is fuel for your productivity.

Spin It: Turning Negative to Positive

The only negative thing that can happen here is for you to sabotage your health. If you blow it and eat half a pack of Oreos, acknowledge your mistake and move on pledging to only eat two next time. If you didn't work out, do a tougher workout tomorrow. If you stayed up all night cramming for a test or watching horror flicks, then go to bed early the next night. The point is to fix where you goof, and not fall into the rut of continually goofing. If you do find yourself down like I was because of constant stress on your health, let it be a wakeup call.

Remember, you are smart, capable and strong. You are worth all of the attention and effort.

Step Three: Self Care Summary

- Remember my story, three weeks down and out with a back injury. Protect yourself.
- Sleep, eat, de-stress every day.
- You need to take care of you to reach your goals, your future, and to take care of those who need you.
- Get caught up on your health, see your doctor, get in top form.
- Organize your time now that you've invigorated your energy/productivity levels.
- Find time for fun.
- If you fall off track, just get back on, no dawdling.

April's Upwords #23

Following the wrong path? Feel like you are meant for a different journey? It's never too late to start over.

Step Four: Re-organize

My Experience

As I walked past the front desk on the way to the elevator, a woman said, “Excuse me, all visitors need to check in please.” She handed me a clipboard with a sign- in sheet that asked for my name, license plate number and make of vehicle, and what floor and office I was going to. I remember thinking; *I can’t believe I have to write this for other people to see.* Ugh. I tried to get an empty elevator car to keep anyone from seeing me exit on the bankruptcy floor, but to no avail. It was a large building with a ton of different types of businesses. I was so embarrassed, sick to my stomach and still in disbelief that it had come to this.

The attorney’s office was at the end of a long corridor. My appointment was at ten o’ clock sharp. I was ten minutes early, thinking I’d get a jump on filling out paperwork or something, but I was mistaken. The entry door was locked and I found myself waiting out in the hall, under a sign that read “BANKRUPTCY.” Double ugh.

I must say I was completely taken by surprise when they

finally opened the door. The offices were bright and sunny. The view of Ann Arbor from the ninth floor was terrific. There were framed pictures on the wall with inspirational sayings, even one of Abraham Lincoln, which depicted how many times he had failed before he became President (two failed businesses and six lost elections between 1831 and 1860). I'd completed my "homework packet" prior and was let into an inner office. For the next hour, a very compassionate, number- savvy attorney guided me through my next three years, explaining the need to lose my house. She said, "We'll get you through this." I burst into tears, right there in her office, mourning the loss of my house, my Beanstalks and my credibility. The tears that seemed to flow the most, however, were tears of relief. Finally I was going to find a way out of this mess.

Stats and Stuff You Need To Know

I can't stress enough the need for an exit strategy when opening up your own business. Why am I so emphatic? Because I didn't have one. This is the one bit of research I didn't really delve into, mostly because I was too naive to think I'd need one. Remember what I mentioned earlier? *What's the worst thing that could happen? We could lose our house?* I never really thought we would.

An exit strategy is a plan to get out of your business and is as important as your plan to get into your business. There are different solutions. You can sell your business to another similar business or franchise. You can set up arrangements on your own to pay everyone you owe, on a payment plan that you can afford, or you can file one of three versions of bankruptcy.

Chapter 7 bankruptcies wipe out everything, give you a clean slate and are the most common type of bankruptcy. A court appointed trustee liquefies all assets and then distributes the proceeds to the creditors. The key here is there is a limit to what you can owe, and you can't have any other means of income.

Chapter 11 bankruptcies are the types we hear about in news headlines from big corporations, most recently, the auto industry. This form of bankruptcy allows a business to reorganize and rehabilitate, allowing the business to restructure and pay off debt from future earnings. Again, this process is overseen by a court appointed trustee.

Lastly is Chapter 13 bankruptcy. This is the umbrella under which we fell. In most cases it is a repayment plan and usually will allow debtors to keep their homes (we lost ours because it was listed as collateral for our business loan). As I stated earlier, I had never been in business before and was considered a risk to the bank and every other leasing company we dealt with inside the business. This meant we were asked to sign a personal guarantee to qualify for any business financing. A personal guarantee is the bank's way of saying, "We'll give you the money, but if you default, we'll come after you personally, as well as professionally." If you are married, or are going to have someone else as a co-signer, the risks are even higher. I specifically remember the day we got the paperwork and the evening Jim and I began to weigh our options. Beanstalks was my baby, my creation. However, the minute we signed the bank's personal guarantee papers, the responsibility became both of ours. Because we were married, the bank wanted all of Jim's financials too. He was also agreeing to risk everything for my ambitious undertaking. If you are married, legally partnered or otherwise with someone, this is the point where you really have to take stock in your relationship. The consequences of something going wrong are no longer only yours to bear. This holds true for whoever is co-signing with you. You have to really discuss whether or not your relationship would survive the devastating results from a failed business. Will your spouse resent you if things get bad? Will you be able to carry the weight of the guilt you will feel if things don't work out? The risks are enormous, but for us were unavoidable. Again, it comes down to making a choice: sign the guarantee and give your dream a go, or don't and well...don't.

I now know the importance of an exit strategy. What would I have done differently if I was to do it all over again? I would have seen the warning signs much sooner and sought out a buyer. For example, the first time I was forced to call my landlord to negotiate rent, or when I saw my customer volume plummet, I should have been putting an exit strategy in place—just in case. As hard as it would have been to hand over the reins of what I had created, at least I would have had an asking price that would've covered my debt. This doesn't mean the first time you can't pay all of your bills you should panic, as many creditors will work with you for a month or two. But when there doesn't seem to be a solution in sight, it is time to seriously figure out how you're going to jump ship, with the least amount of casualties possible.

Why This Step (Re-organize) Is So Important

There is something to be said about de-cluttering your life. I don't know about you, but I have a catch-all basket in my dining room that seems to have a life of its own. I know enough to realize the "stuff" in the basket is everything I don't want to deal with. It is either time consuming, or emotionally haunting, or maybe I'm just saving it "just in case" I'll use it or need it later. Then, after procrastinating long enough, or receiving a gentle nudge from my husband (who deals with most of the "stuff" for us both), I finally tackle "my pile".

Cleaning up after your business, however, is not the same as putting off calling the insurance company about a discrepancy on your last bill or waiting on "robot hold" to make an appointment for your dog. If you put off the insurance company for a month, you'll still be able to see the doctor if you get the flu, and your dog will get groomed soon enough. Put off all of the loose ends from your business and you won't be able to get on with your life. You'll be stuck in a span of motionlessness, with a mountain of legal trouble and unable to move forward to the future awaiting you. You know how you feel when you clean off your desk? Organized, accomplished, and inspired? Now multiply that feeling by one million.

Take Action TODAY

(just take it one hour at a time, this is time consuming but necessary)

1. Call your attorney. If you don't have one (gasp!) then find one, figure out which exit strategy is for you.
2. Call all your services and contractors, banks and creditors, to let them know you are closing up and how you are doing it. This is especially true if you are filing for bankruptcy because the creditors will want to start legal work of their own. Then thank them for their services (yep, you read correctly, *thank them*).
3. Call your tax preparer. If you don't have one (double gasp!) find one. See **Practical Advice** below.

4. Send thank you cards to every contact, customer and colleague who supported you. Tell them you are going out of business, but wouldn't have been able to accomplish all that you did without their support. I can't stress enough the importance of never burning bridges.

List of people to notify once a business is closing: *(utilities, delivery services, inventory, banks, credit cards, vendors, maintenance, landlords, supporters, etc.)*

Company	Contact	Phone	Date Notified	Thank you Sent?

Practical Advice

Unless you are an accountant, or work for "the Block" during tax season, you need a tax preparer. You'll need to make sure you are current on Federal, State and City taxes of all sorts. Property taxes are usually prorated so, for example, you won't pay last quarter taxes until June of the following year. This tripped me up because I closed up shop in January, and got a new bill in June. Also, if applicable, you'll need to deal with sales and payroll taxes too, and these can be very complicated. Finally, put your manager's cap back on and make sure your employees get their W-2's.

One lesson I learned the hard way, is you should try to keep one company or tax prep service throughout your entire time in business, and after. Originally, I had a large payroll company taking care of all of my tax needs. They did a fantastic job and I never had to give my taxes a thought (until I had to pay them!). Eventually, however, I could no longer afford the larger company's service fees, so I switched to our personal tax preparer (Super Kath!). This is not to say that each of them weren't stellar representatives in their fields, it just made matters a bit confusing after the close of the business when trying to figure out who filed what, especially when I had been behind on everything.

My advice, don't mess with the IRS, but don't fear them either. If I have learned one thing about taxes, it is the government will go out of its way to help you balance out. I know it sounds surprising, but I've seen example after example, in addition to my own experience, where patience exercised by the Internal Revenue Service has been a reality. This does not mean, however, you can wait to start making arrangements. As long as you are making the effort, the IRS will work with you. Skip out though, and you will undoubtedly suffer the very real, legal consequences.

Feed Your Energy

It always feels better to do the right thing. Clear the slate. Filing bankruptcy certainly wasn't my proudest moment, but it really gave me a path to follow, and way of paying back *something*. I had formed respectable business relationships with my creditors and truly felt awful for not being able to pay them in full. At least with Chapter 13 I was doing what I could. A clear conscience in business is the same as a clear conscience in life. Do your absolute best and the guilt will stay away.

Secondly, be professional and gracious. You want people to remember you as the person who held her/his head high. I'll never forget an evening in February 2009, only a month after Beanstalks had closed. I was working an event in our downtown district when I came upon a couple of ladies having dinner at the corner grille. They asked me how I was doing. I remember saying, "thank you ladies, it has been really challenging, but I'm looking ahead to what I'm going to do next," then proceeded to tell them I was thinking of focusing on my writing career. I wish I had a photo of their faces. They were in disbelief, completely shocked and impressed that I could be looking forward only a month after the business had collapsed. Keep your eye on your next prize and people will take note of your positive attitude and give you kudos for it. They will also keep you in mind should some kind of prospect come their way that is suitable to you in the future.

Spin It: Turning Negative to Positive

Losing my house, my family's home, was like getting punched in the face. It wasn't long though before the emotional bruises began to heal, and believe it or not, I started finding things wrong with my house. A psychologist might say this was my way of dealing with the separation anxiety that would come with a move, but it helped me nonetheless. I continually found good reasons, and even benefits, to downsizing. I shared these revelations with my husband and sons too in hopes of taking away the loss they would feel. I didn't disrespect all of the wonderful memories we shared there, I just didn't dwell on them. My family didn't deny the pain; we just chose to really focus on the future. Downsizing was the necessary step to the next great thing. And you better believe, with three sets of eyes following my lead, I was more determined than ever to make a future that would guarantee their happiness.

Step Four: Re-Organize Summary

- Remember my story--the ride up the elevator got easier.
- Find your exit strategy, how will you pay your creditors?
- Recognize the benefits of de-cluttering your life.
- Make your calls to let people know you are out of business, thank them.
- Deal with taxes, it is the law.
- Do the right thing, don't leave loose ends.
- Help those around you to deal with the loss.

April's Upwords # 21

You know there is something you have always dreamed of doing. No excuses. Find a way. Just thinking about it will motivate you.

Think, then DO.

Step Five: The Next Great Thing

Note: Now comes the fun part. This is when you begin to think what it is you want to do next, what excites you, which direction you will go. From here on out you will identify your mission and be guided along your path. We do this by taking what we've learned from our past mistakes, and using that new knowledge to leap forward.

My Experience:

After all that I have experienced in business and all I have studied and read since my business closed, I am a real believer of "you get what you see", as opposed to "you see what you get." When I first got fired up about Beanstalks, it was a continuously playing film in my head. I was so excited about it! Throughout the day I was planning and inquiring. Before I went to sleep at night I decorated the building for it in my mind. I knew what colors would be on which wall. I knew what it would look like, what music would play and how I would welcome my guests. The more I thought about it, the clearer it became and the more exciting it was...and I literally felt the excitement and adrenaline every time I thought about it.

What I didn't know at the time was that I was programming myself for success, creating what I call a *future picture*. I didn't wish for Beanstalks to become a reality, I was planning on it. I *knew* it was coming, just didn't know when. You may ask, how did I know? I wanted it so badly that I just behaved and acted as if it was a done deal, before I even told my husband, let alone called a bank! I positively knew I would be successful in opening my business, and trusted all of the pieces would fall into place...and they did. It wasn't hocus pocus. I didn't click my heels three times and wish for funding, the lease or the customers. It's just that the more I believed in the outcome, the more resourceful I became in finding what I needed, what I call *positive knowing*.

That having been said, you might be wondering why then, did I end up losing it? Knowing what I now know, it is clear to me what the beginning of the end was. I let myself get really scared. The more freaked out I was, the more self-doubt crept in. Looking back, I wonder where in the world my passion and excitement went? At what point did I say to myself, "April, you are failing"? When did I decide to let the fear kill the drive, and why didn't I use the same inner guidance and resources to keep my business going as I did to get it open? The problem was I didn't know what tools I had used to fire me up in the first place, they were just there. I didn't know how detrimental fear could be. I wasn't aware then the role of my emotions and how they would direct my hand without me even recognizing it. I've since found clarity. I have studied the thoughts and read the books of successful people. They all share a common thread. They see what they want, and they get it. And it is happening for me again too.

Once I got off the couch and cleaned up the last lingerings of

Beanstalks, I began to think about what I wanted next. It took me awhile to find what I was looking for, something that really excited me. I would write ideas down, search the internet for anything that caught my attention. Did I want to try another play café? Did I want a different kind of retail business? I began thinking of what I was good at, what I enjoyed doing in my free time. It took considerable time but looking back as far as I could remember, I was a writer. I won contests as a kid. I had always taken classes on how to write in different genres, and here's the key, I took those classes *just for fun*! When I was off work for maternity leave, both times, I would dawdle with writing. I had so many journals around my house it rivaled the stationary section of a bookstore. Hmmm….Beanstalks was modeled around storybooks and children's authors. My favorite event to volunteer for at my son's school was "March Is Reading Month". All of my college courses gravitated toward composition and literature. At the very least, this information was insightful.

I started writing letters to the editor of the local paper, or short articles of local importance. I began thinking about how other businesses might be struggling, or how they are surviving, and wanted to write about that. Time and time again I found myself at my keyboard. The wheels had begun to turn. The final, confirming moment for me was the first time I saw my by-line in print. I was so excited, so energized, so motivated to keep writing. Getting credit for something I write is a blast, but the real powerful part of it for me was the fact that I could write about issues of importance to me, and spread them to the masses. I continued with articles, made myself available as a freelancer, created five blogs on different topics, and before I knew it had a following. That was the beginning, but not yet what I "saw" in the movie in my head.

This time, as I sat at my home computer, writing and blogging and thinking, I started to see another future picture. It is me on a stage in an auditorium, speaking to people about my experience in business, and about the book I had written (this book!). In my picture I'm at numerous locations signing and selling books. I'm at schools reading and doing activities around children's titles I have written. I'm at my husband's retirement party because I'm successful enough so that he can pursue his own future picture.

I make a point to see my future picture, run the film in my head every chance I get throughout each and every day. I have tools to help me see it. I add sound and color and any other senses that seem to fit. And guess what? This book has happened. The speaking has begun. I am quickly on my way to "getting what I see" once again.

Stats and Stuff You Need to Know

The first thing I hear from many people when I mention positive thinking as an actual activity is that they consider it the same as wishful thinking, and that there isn't a silver lining to every situation. As I'm sure you've figured out by now by reading thus far, I believe there is indeed a silver lining to every situation because even the most awful of circumstances have lessons for us to learn once we survive them. And, wishful thinking is nothing like positive thinking, or as I prefer, *positive knowing.* I'm not alone; research on the benefits of positive thinking has erupted over the past decade. You may consider the process of positive thinking as a self-affirming academic exercise, a more faith based and prayer-like method, or even new-age universalism that monitors energy. All of these include a belief system, and with strong beliefs comes emotional commitment, which is a key player in "getting what you see". Whichever way you interpret the process, some scientific and medical communities are weighing in on the side of success.

We've been hearing for years how a positive outlook may aid in the healing of cancer patients. In fact, there are brick and mortar, independent health care centers with entire departments devoted to mindful thinking. The James Graham Brown Cancer Center (University of Louisville) concentrates on Behavioral Oncology and the roles of mindfulness and meditation as effective treatments of cancer and fibromyalgia. Within their cancer screening and prevention research studies sector, they study patient's attitudes, beliefs and responses. Mind over matter when it comes to battling cancer is a controversial subject; however, there is significant agreement and evidence that optimism has a benefit on the immune system. This in turn helps the body fight off a variety of illnesses, whereas a negative attitude can do the opposite. A study in 2003 at the University of Wisconsin reported people subjected to the flu vaccine fared worse if they had higher activity levels in the part of the brain that is activated by negative emotions. The opposing argument seems to be that benefits from a positive attitude may be attributed to the idea that positive minded people tend to take better care of their health in general, thus have a better chance of preventing illness and disease compared to people who do not take care of their health.

While researching the effects of positive thinking on overall health, I came across an article in the Review of General Psychology written by Shelly L. Gable of the University of California, Los Angeles and Jonathan Haidt from the University of Virginia. The article is titled "What (and Why) Is Positive Psychology?" and explores the study of healthy mindedness, or "the study of the conditions and processes that contribute to the flourishing or optimal functioning of people, groups and institutions." The authors talk about a positive psychology *movement*. The idea is not to deny the existence of "human suffering, selfishness, dysfunctional family systems and ineffective institutions" but to study the opposite, "the ways that people feel joy, show altruism, and create healthy families and institutions." By studying areas of human experience like love, hope, inspiration, curiosity, forgiveness and laughter, they seek a balance of the everyday human condition.

The most important thing to note, as was confirmed in almost every publication and study I researched, was the fact that positive thinking must be sincere. In fact, those who didn't genuinely believe in what they were thinking, found trying too hard or faking a positive outlook to be a stressor, the opposite of the intended outcome. Bottom line, if you do not believe wholeheartedly in your future picture, or that the movie in your brain indeed exists for you, you are less likely to find yourself in the starring role you seek.

Why This Step (The Next Great Thing) Is So Important

We all need a starting point. Not just any starting point, but one that excites us! Remember when we were children in school and we were asked what we wanted to be when we grew up? We never said, "I'd say I want to be an astronaut but I know that's not going to happen." We said, "I'm going to go to the moon someday!" We didn't hesitate, we were limitless. Truly, we believed we could be anything we wanted unless someone told us different. Maybe it was a science teacher who told a girl in his class that girls weren't as good in science as boys. Maybe it was an uncle who told his nephew that he didn't belong in college, but instead was meant for the family business. Dreams were sabotaged without us even realizing what had happened. So many people are constantly told what they *can't* do, that they don't even consider the options for what they *can* do.

Guess what? YOU CAN. Start thinking, dreaming and exploring the possibilities for yourself. There are no limits to what you can seek, learn and accomplish. You are smart, capable and worthy.

One of my favorite movies is called "Freedom Writers". It is a true story about a rookie English teacher named Erin Gruwell, who takes a group of inner city students and teaches them they are worthy of success, despite their pre-stamped dispositions to achieve nothing. There is a scene in the film where Mrs. Gruwell is welcoming her sophomores back to school after summer vacation. She gives them new books in Borders bags, and sparkling cider in plastic wine glasses. She then recites to them a "Toast For Change".

"From this moment on, every voice that told you 'you can't' is silenced. Every reason that tells you things will never change disappears. And the person you were before this moment, that person's turn is over. Now it's your turn."--Erin Gruwell

I love that scene and I believe in her message. It *is* your turn. Find what inspires you, gives you joy and fires you up. That's your start. Let's go!

Take Action TODAY

(take as much time as you need here, keep evolving)

1. Self assess. Make a list of what you enjoy even if you aren't good at it. What makes you happy? Gets you excited? Let your list speak to you. The one group of words, you keep going back to...that's where you need to go to find your next career.

Self Assessment/Dream Page

If I could pick any profession in the entire world, no matter what it would take to do it, I would

---

My favorite hobbies are

The most exciting trip I can imagine taking would be

I am so good at

If I had to teach something to someone, I would teach

My role models are *(business or personal)*

2. Make a vision board. See my "How to Make a Vision Board" at the end of this chapter.

3. What is your future picture? Start playing your movie in your head. Picture yourself doing exactly what you want to be doing, remember, you are smiling and successful at whatever it is. Play your movie as many times a day as you can. Pretty soon your subconscious will play it for you, kind of like background music.

Practical Advice

Some people might really have a hard time buying into the "getting what you see" process. That's okay. I was leery too, until I studied the concept, then ultimately experienced it working. Here are some books that go a bit deeper, describe the process and give more and more examples of its success. These are what I read and still read again and again.

Think and Grow Rich by Napolean Hill. (I keep this book in my purse!)
"As A Man Thinketh" by James Allen
The 7 Habits of Highly Effective People by Stephen Covey
The Slight Edge by Jeff Olson (simplifies the choices we make each day--great!)
How To Get What You Want and Want What You Have by John Gray
Your Best Life Now by Joel Osteen (for those of you looking for something faith based)
The Secret by Rhonda Byrne (for those more universalist/energy minded)

I've Seen a Lot of People Naked, and They've Got Nothing on You by Jake Steinfeld (a real focus on risk-taking)

The Worry Trap by Chad Lejeune, Ph. D. (get rid of your anxiety NOW)...thanks Nathan!

52 Simple Ways to Build Your Child's Self-Esteem & Confidence by Jan Dargatz (don't give kids the "can't" complex, lead them to success early!)

Anything written by Bob Proctor. The man is the master in positively training your thoughts.

Feed Your Energy

Positive knowing. Future Picture. Movie in your head. Vision Boards and other tools. All of these things play a role in re-training the way you think. You must remember, however, these tools take you nowhere unless you *feel.* It's all about emotion. So how do you do that? The easiest way to feel the emotions of what you envision is to act as if you are already there. If you want to be a business owner, act like one, dress like one, talk like one. Whatever it is you want to be or do, start taking the steps to get there. When I made the first call to the realtor about the castle building for Beanstalks, I didn't say, "Hello. I've never had a business before but I was wondering if I could see the place." Instead, I said, "Hello. My name is April Scarlett and I am actively seeking a location for my business." Feel the difference? Can you see how I might stand up straighter and carry myself with more confidence with the second option? You have to *be the dream* so that it becomes your reality. Feel free to grant yourself that new identity. This doesn't mean, however, being nonsensical. If you want to be a pilot, you aren't going to step onto an airplane and say, "Hello, I'm a pilot". If your future picture is you as a pilot, then most certainly you are taking flying lessons and you can say, "Hello, my name is _________ and I have _____hours in the air towards getting my license. Would it be okay if I observed today's flight?" Homeland security might have something to say about this on a commercial flight, but there are a lot of private companies who just might take you up on it. You won't know if you don't ask. Don't be afraid to embrace what it is you want, the emotion will fall into place. You'll be so excited about taking a step, the enthusiasm, adrenaline and simple happiness will flood in automatically.

Spin It: Turning Negative to Positive

You may have a tough time zeroing in on what it is you want your future picture to be. Be patient with yourself. Just keep jotting down ideas. When it is right you will know it. Take this obstacle as an opportunity to explore all of the things you enjoy. If you don't turn one of them into a career path, perhaps you'll make time to incorporate them into other areas of your life.

There will be people who think you are wasting your time "daydreaming." Don't give them the power to discourage you. There are always going to be naysayers and others who do not agree with anything you do. Take the high road. Respect their opinion and then let them keep it for themselves. It's important not to get defensive, which is a symptom of frustration. Keep the negativity at bay.

Every obstacle is an opportunity to learn something new, put something behind you, block negativity and lead you to your next great thing. Use obstacles as tools, then they are no longer obstacles, they are stepping stones. The formula is:

obstacles divided by learned knowledge equals stepping stone.

O/LK=SS.

Step Five: The Next Great Thing Summary

- Remember my experience, twice I've put the future picture in my head, twice it has worked.
- Learn and embrace the power of positive thinking, do your research, clear away any doubts, read, read, read!
- Self assess, use tools to figure out what it is you want, start making the movie in your head.
- *Feel* your future picture, act as if you are already starring in your future role, let the emotion flourish.
- Use obstacles as stepping stones to what is next for you.

Special Project: How to Make a Vision Board

A vision board is a spectacular tool. It gives you something to look at, to really see yourself in your future picture. The best part is they are FUN to make.

What you'll need:

- A piece of cardboard or poster board, any kind of cardstock paper, any size you like, I'd say at least 11 x 17.
- Magazines, photos, maps, clip art from the computer…any visual aid of what you want for yourself
- Glue, scissors

The object is to incorporate yourself into a future picture. Clip out things you like, don't be afraid of appearing materialistic…this is just a tool. What kind of house do you want to live in? What car will you drive? Where will you travel? Put photos of the important people in your life that you plan on sharing it with. If you don't have anyone yet, but hope to have loved ones in the future, cut hearts or flowers or a wedding dress/tuxedo. If you want more money, find pictures of money. For me, I want to get my books published so I have photos of books.

Vision Board by April Scarlett

When I made my vision board, I wanted to use it to its maximum potential. In a picture of a spectacular home office, I scanned photos of my kids, shrunk them down on my computer and put them in the photos that hung on the wall in the cut out. I took pictures of items on my real desk, shrunk them and inset them into the cut out photo. I took a picture of myself, shrunk it, put my head on a body about 4 sizes smaller than my own in a stellar business suit and leaned it up next to a new Cadillac. The sky is the limit! Dream it and cut it and then glue it on your vision board in any form you like. Mine is kind of like a collage, but you can keep yours linear if you like. There are no rules, just cut and glue and have fun. Keep adding to it each time you find something new that you love.

As soon as you've started your vision board, even if it only has one picture on it at the onset, put it in a place where you see it every day. I keep mine above my desk because I am ALWAYS at my desk. I know people who have theirs in their kitchen, or on their bedside table, even near the bathroom mirror. I also scanned my vision board into a computer file so when I'm really feeling a lack of motivation, I set it as my wallpaper on my computer monitor!

April's Upwords # 35

You have all the power you need. You just have to use it.

Step Six: Plan

My Experience

I had decided that I wanted to take my writing to the next level. Up to this point I had been writing here and there, but not getting paid for it. I had to decide what plan of action I would take to bring in money while doing what I love. I was smart enough to know this would not happen overnight. Again, no hocus pocus. I had to think it out, concentrate on my future picture and take the steps needed to get me to my starring role.

First of all, I knew nobody would pay me to write if they didn't know whether or not I could do it well. I continued to write for free, or for a very small amount so I would have clips, or published pieces of work, to show a new client, editor or publication. In addition to proving my skill, I had to show I could write on a broad range of topics and could research and interview well. And if I was short on a skill, I needed to brush up. This meant checking out the latest publishing software for newsletters and brochures, learning the latest Search Engine Optimization for web content, and deciding if I was going to try my hand at technical writing, which would take some college courses.

Next, I had to let people know I was available. I researched the going rates for freelance writers in different regions of the country, largely based on years of experience, and drew up a rate sheet that was appropriate. I updated my résumé and sent the rate sheet, résumé and clips to editors, publications and business contacts. I let business networks I was in know what I was up to. I'll never forget the first time I mentioned it at a Downtown Merchant Meeting. It was the first meeting I had attended since losing Beanstalks. The group meets every other week and I had probably missed three meetings. I was welcomed back graciously and took the opportunity to let people know what I was planning to do next. Honestly, these were good people, I had a good rapport with them and if I hadn't offered up my plans, they would have asked anyway. At the end of the meeting, the City manager took me aside and said he thought there might be some writing work available for the City, and that he'd be in touch. This was the first time I had even breathed a word about my writing business and I already had a potential client! This is where networks really come in handy. When you build a trustworthy relationship with a colleague, contractor or customer, it will only help you in your later endeavors. Again, this is about not burning bridges and giving back to those around you. Everything comes full circle. I cannot emphasize enough the importance of maintaining a reputation of respect, professionalism, trust and community.

Finally, I had to decide what kind of business I wanted to build, and what I was allowed to do legally while in my three years of bankruptcy since the loss of Beanstalks (more homework). And then the final piece of the puzzle, I needed to put it all out on paper in the form of a business plan. With a stroke of a pen and a few business cards and calls, April Scarlett the freelance writer, became ASW April Scarlett Writes.

Stats and Stuff You Need to Know

Organization is key. You have to build your empire one brick at a time, in perfect balance, with just enough bricks and the right amount of mortar. You have to draw it up, engineer it and see the outcome before you even start. Some people use spreadsheets, some have hundreds of sticky notes all over a bulletin board. I used a tool I learned while going through a terrific program called the Saline Leadership Institute. One day per month for one year, my classmates and I were privy to the advice and lessons of experts in leadership, business and community. We attended seminars on everything from personality traits management to team building. This is where I met Jamie Nast.

Jamie is an international expert and author of Idea Mapping. As defined on her website (www.ideamappingsuccess.com), "Idea Mapping is a powerful, whole-brained thinking tool that enhances memory, note-taking skills, thought organization, planning, creativity and communication. It uses color, key words, lines and images to connect thoughts associatively. Idea Maps are the natural expression of the way the brain processes information associatively." I can't say enough about this process. I like to think of it as the creative side of my brain working with my more analytical side, together, to get me to where I need to be faster and more efficiently. Here is an example of one of my maps on platform (step 8 is entirely on platform).

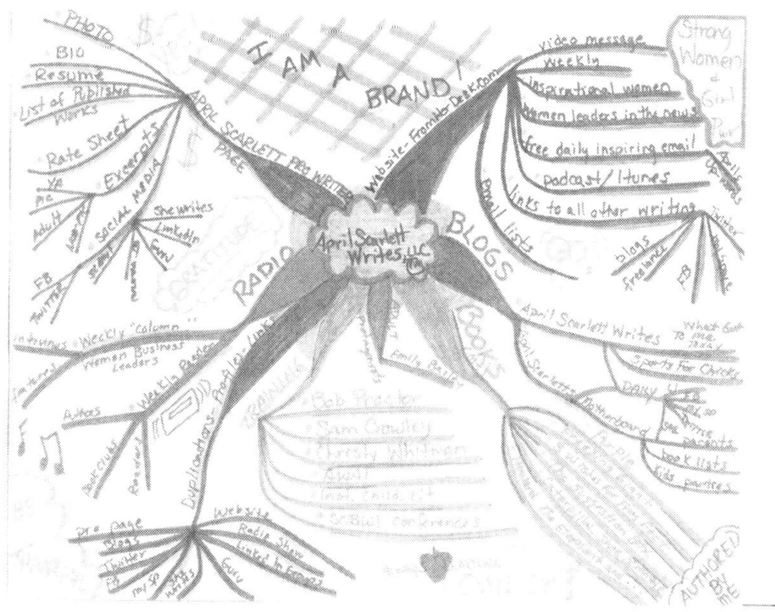

You can see in the middle is the name of my company. Outstretched from the center are branches, each of a different color, representing each of the different ways I plan to promote myself. You see my website, blogs, books, adult fiction, profiles and links, training, radio, and my pro writer page. From each of these branches stems smaller lines, depicting the details of each one. They are all in their own color, which helps me remember each one. Even when I'm not looking at the map, when I think about my books, I see the orange in my head, which helps me remember the rest of the orange/book information. This is where the associations come in. My creative side sees the color, and matches it up with the informational side. The rest of the map shows pictures or words I associate with the information. Some maps don't have words at all and are one hundred percent illustrations.

It is an exciting exercise and tool that is fun and easy to do.

There is no wrong way of doing it, and no two maps are the same. If you aren't a crayons and markers kind of person, there is computer software to follow. Think of an Idea Map as a flow chart on vacation. It still shows you where to go and what to do; it just lets you have a lot more fun getting there! Idea mapping is a perfect tool to help you see where you are going and your map will hang nicely next to your vision board. Visit Jamie's website and read her book to learn how to create your own Idea Map for success.

Speaking of organization, as soon as you begin preparing and moving into your future picture, you'll start accumulating piles of "stuff": information on demographics, research into your field, papers of incorporation or emails from mentors, website printouts from government sites and piles of books to read. Get yourself organized. Make files, keep records of all communications, and get some form of rolodex or business card album. Try and keep your desk or dining room table (wherever you are working) in order. Believe me, I know this is a tough one, just ask my kids who like to do their homework at my desk and often can't find room to write. But it is worth the time and effort to keep it tidy. When a business contact, banker or contractor calls, you want to be able to pull up their information immediately so you can fully participate in the conversation. There are countless resources online and at the bookstore to help you combat clutter. I'll tell you what, you do it and I will too!

Why This Step (Plan) Is So Important

Everything you are doing up to this point keeps you moving forward. Preparation is your best defense against coming to a halt.

Remember the obstacles we talked about? It is true, any obstacle can be spun to be a stepping stone, but if we don't have obstacles to spin, we'll get to where we are going a lot faster.

Planning and preparation also keeps us current. When an opportunity comes along to move you closer to your future picture (and it will), it is essential you are ready. I came across a quote by famous illustrator Henry Hartman (Lone Ranger artist) that sums up this concept perfectly. He said, "Success always comes when preparation meets opportunity." Clearly he is correct. Take my work for example, if an editor calls me and needs somebody to write a small biography, I'm a step ahead of my competition if I've got a clip of a similar piece of work, have proven my interviewing skills and have a good reference for her to call. What if you want to open your own tax service business and receive a call from a reputable accounting firm looking to hire someone temporarily for the tax season? Will you outshine your competition if you are up to speed on the newest tax laws and changes, both for individuals and small businesses? You will if you have been preparing. Think of what a brief stint at such a reputable firm will do for your resume!

Preparation of this kind comes even before the business plan. You can never be too prepared, and preparation never really stops. As you get further along in your success, you will find new goals that require new research and on and on and on. Continuous planning is the key to keeping current in your field and above the competition.

Take Action TODAY

(20 minutes to 2 hours)

1. Write down three steps you can take this week. For example, call

about schooling/training or an internship, inquire about child care if you need to. What are the costs? Have your eye on a location? Call and ask about it.

2. Locate a possible mentor in your field and ask if you could buy them a cup of coffee to pick their brain. Don't be shy. Most people will be flattered and happy to chat with you for fifteen to thirty minutes, and when they say yes, be prompt and follow up with a thank you note
3. Take a day to drive around to similar businesses like the one you want to open, take notes about what you like and what you don't, add it to your research file.
4. Check out Idea Mapping to learn how to use this valuable learning tool

Use this space to organize your first steps. Don't wait! Your future picture is counting on you.

Today's Date:_______________

Three steps I will take this week to move my plans forward:

1. ____

2. ____

3. ____

A mentor in my field is: _______________________________

The contact info for this person is: ____________________

Meeting time and date is: ______________________________

Date this list will be completed by: _____________________

Practical Advice

I can't talk about planning without emphasizing the importance of having a business plan. Before you mentally check out from boredom or intimidation, let me tell you it is not as bad as you think. There are lots of books and tools to help you through it, and software that literally takes you key stroke by keystroke; you don't even have to be a techie. Or if you really break out in hives just thinking about it, for enough money there are people who will write up a business plan for you (wink wink, my rates are competitive). Think of your business plan as your ticket to opportunity. It not only gives you a standard to refer to later as you go about building your business, but there isn't a bank in existence who will lend you the money without it. Because there are so many resources, I'll give you the basics and then you can choose your own method for creating your individual business plan.

A business plan is your pitch. It is a tool that sells your idea on paper. This is when your idea really takes shape, and looks like something that is real, as opposed to a thought in your head only you know about. It begins with an Executive Summary.

An Executive summary is just what it sounds like. It is you, the executive, summarizing what your business concept is all about. It highlights what is special about your idea and why customers will choose it. It introduces what is included in the document and the purpose of the plan. The Executive Summary includes the objectives of your proposed business, a mission statement, and the major components that will lead to your company's success.

The next part of the business plan contains information about the legal set up of your business. It includes a company summary, legal entity identity (individual, partnership, S-corp, et al), and summary of estimated start-up costs. Then you'll detail your products and services, which is what you offer and what you will charge for it.

By far the most research intensive part of the plan, at least for me, was the next section concerning the market analysis for your business and competition. Here you must explain not only who your market is, but break it down into demographics and how your location and mission fit the market you are seeking to reach, and then how you plan to reach it. You also must identify specific competition, and do a market comparison that shows why your product or service outshines the competition and will be strong enough to both lure customers and clients your way, or at the very least share with those in the same business, especially if they are in a close location geographically. What gives your company a competitive edge?

Further with marketing, you'll need to describe your website planning, costs and implementation. How else will you market? What will your strategy be? You should do a S.W.O.T Analysis (Strengths, Weaknesses, Opportunities, Threats) and report on each.

The second half of the business plan is all about money. You need to forecast your sales. In other words, how are you going to make money? You will discuss management, personnel, projected profit and loss, break even analysis (at what point you will break even and start earning a profit), cash flow projections and a balance sheet. If any of these sounds foreign to you, like they did to me in the beginning, then you need to do some homework or enlist the help of someone who is good with these kinds of numbers.

Business plans can seem overwhelming. Don't be afraid to ask for help. The better understanding you have of all aspects of your business, from creative to financial, the better prepared you'll be when opportunity comes knocking.

Feed Your Energy

All of this planning and research can be overwhelming. Don't forget the things we discussed in steps two and three about taking care of yourself. Pace is also important. Nothing is created overnight. What is that saying about building Rome, is it, in a day? Pace and timing are why we have steps to follow in the first place. Take one at a time, and don't beat yourself up if you need a break. As a matter of fact, I encourage you to take breaks so you can re-energize. I do this with writing all of the time. If I'm working on a lengthy piece, sometimes I get so caught up in it that I'll write for hours, late into the evening, until my eyes are buggy and my brain is slow and foggy. It only took one mistake for me to realize the importance of taking a breather. I was working on a story for the local paper, covering the budget for the school board. It was a pretty hot-button issue for the time and there were a lot of details. I knew my editor wanted the article sooner than later, so after the board meeting, I stayed up writing about it until about 2:00 AM. When I was finally done, I saved the file for myself, and emailed a copy to my editor. You can imagine my horror the next morning when I reviewed the article and found loads of mistakes! There were spelling errors, grammatical errors, and paragraphs which had no business even being in the piece. I was mortified because I knew I had already submitted my work. I had to edit the article and re-submit it, and apologize for the quality of the work, explaining how I had worked late into the evening (no excuse). It was unprofessional at best. Luckily, the editor was fairly familiar with my writing and it didn't make too much of an impact on my reputation. I still get queasy when I think what might have happened if I had done that to an editor or publication who was reading my work for the first time!

Take as many breaks as you need. Exercise, rest, play, whatever it takes to renew your energy so you can get back to doing productive work.

Spin It: Turning Negative to Positive

Not everyone is going to love your idea, but if you keep going you will find someone who will. Most of the time, it seems there is a reason to finding just the right time and place for an opportunity. I have countless examples of this. Take a lovely woman named Jessica. She is a mother of four who was raising her children and worked at home as a medical transcriptionist until her job was outsourced overseas. Jess was very intimidated to go back to college and pursue her dream of becoming a nurse. The first time she went to a nearby college guidance office to ask where to begin, she was treated rudely, condescendingly, and was completely discouraged. She left questioning whether or not nursing was really in her future anyway. Thankfully she didn't quit. She went to another school, found a different counselor who not only encouraged her but helped her make a plan, both for course of study and financial aid. Jessica went on to excel in her studies, continuously making the Dean's list; she survived a brutal nursing program, and will graduate later this year with honors. Not only is she now an excellent nurse, she has set her sights on more education and an even higher goal in her field. I know this story so well because Jessica is my daughter-in-law, and I've watched her exceed all of her expectations, even after that first counselor all but slammed the door in her face.

I am another example. It took six banks telling me no for a business loan, before I found one to tell me yes. Again, the six obstacles turned into stepping stones, because each made me re-think what was realistic for my business. Closed doors are not roadblocks; they are simply detours sending you in a better direction.

Step Six: Plan Summary

- Remember my story, show what you've got, don't be shy when it comes to showcasing your abilities.
- Get organized, try any method you like, I really like Idea Mapping.
- Prepare, prepare, prepare.
- Find three things to do to further you along your path.
- Write your business plan.
- Don't get overwhelmed, take breaks when you need to refresh.
- Don't take no for an answer, be encouraged, keep trying when something or someone doesn't like your idea, whatever you do, do not give up.

April's Upwords #6

Do one thing today that gets you closer to your dream. Sleep. Wake. Repeat.

Step Seven: Networking

My experience

I was ready to roll in the world of writing. The absolutely most essential thing I can point out about what got me work sooner than later, was the people I knew and the relationships I had formed with them. Over the course of the past two years I had met countless people, all in one form of business or another. Not only had I met them, I had some sort of business relationship with them. This meant I might've attended one of their events at their business, taken time out to see what it is they do. I might know their kid just got braces because they told me so when I set up my grocery order of caramel candy and Starbursts. One of my best clients is my son's former preschool; you bet I approached them too. I was comfortable that everyone I knew, because of my previous experience working with them, would either inquire about me writing for them or give me a referral if the need came up.

It happens all the time. Into my inbox, "Hello, my name is so and so and someone else referred you for a writing project. Are you available to discuss our needs?" or, "Do you have some examples of your work you could send", or "I saw a newsletter for so and so and was wondering if you could do ours too?" Other emails or calls come from editors of nearby newspapers who received my contact information from editors I work with.

None of these connections would have been made if I had been a jerk to work with, or had not taken an interest in those I came across. It's like the delivery driver who brought me my inventory. If I treated him terribly, or was rude or dismissive, on the day when it was raining out do you think he would've made any extra effort to keep my boxes of stuff dry? It's the same with any business or customer connection you make. I knew my delivery driver's name, knew he had just named his newborn son after his favorite football team, and took an interest in his daily existence. I treated him with respect, and in turn he did the same. As is the case with every other person I came into contact with. Respect is everything. This doesn't mean everyone likes me, I'm sure I drive some people up the wall. But I do know there isn't any one contact I am aware of in my business history, who would say I wasn't fair, respectable and honest. These are the characteristics that get me my referrals.

Stats and Stuff You Need to Know

It is like the diner down the street that is a real dive. It's a no muss, no fuss greasy spoon without anything shiny, gimmicky or modern and yet it is packed with customers every morning from 6:00 am to noon. People don't flock there because of the ambiance, and maybe the food is just standard. It's packed because customers feel at home there, they are treated like friends and family, they have formed relationships with the owners, employees, and even other customers. I am not saying a lousy product can be sweetened by good conversation, I'm just pointing out the impact good relationships can have on business.

There is a lot of information available for business relationship building strategies. Business magazines often feature articles about the subject, sometimes quarterly. Communication skills, understandably, top the list of how-to's when it comes to talking business. How often do you reach out to your clients? What tone of voice do you use? What about body language and timing of pitch? Suddenly, talking to a client doesn't seem so simple. The trick is to consider all of these factors and still be genuine.

I like to keep in touch with my writing clients, and be available to them for other resources too. This is where community involvement can really be beneficial to your business relationship. A client might need me to do some writing for them, but they also know if they have another question about connecting to their community, where to find a specific service, who to call to complain about a zoning issue or where to obtain entry forms for the holiday parade, they can call me. Some people might say, "I don't have time for that! I'm busy enough just doing my job, running my business." Understood. However, if you are in the position of being a resource, not only is it a way to give back to your customer in appreciation for their business, but it keeps you visible even when your services aren't needed. My clients don't forget me in between writing projects, and this keeps me at the front of their radar when it's time for a new newsletter. Business relationships are all about give and take, trust and acceptance. I serve my customers well, and I know they will do the same for me in return.

Sometimes when we are all wrapped up in our pitch and enthusiasm for our product or service, we forget to listen to whom we are communicating with. This is a big mistake. There isn't a business partner, investor or customer out there who isn't looking for something from you, just as you are looking for something from them. You must listen to the needs and wants of those you interact with. This doesn't mean having to put up with an elevator pitch thrown upon you by a stranger at a networking event (see Practical Advice), but you do need to know whether or not what you are offering is something the other person needs. If they don't, the key is to make enough of an impression that they will refer you or call you themselves when the need arises. For example, you might own a dry cleaning business and strike up a conversation with the owner of a plumbing company. The plumbers who work for him aren't required to be in uniform, and even if they were they probably would be wash and wear. Obviously, this guy doesn't really have a need for your business. This doesn't mean you shouldn't continue a conversation with him. Ask about his business, what kinds of things he's in need of. Maybe you have a connection you could pass along to help him find what he needs (of course, you will write this contact on the back of *your* business card). Know that networking is not about take, take, take. It is about helping, trust and dependability. At the end of your conversation you will give him your business card and wish him the best, maybe follow up with him to see if the referral you gave worked out and show you respect the business he is in. You better believe the first time this plumbing company owner comes across a client or colleague or company in need of a dry cleaner, the referral will be for you!

Why This Step (Networking) Is So Important

You will not succeed in business if you try and do everything solo. I can't stress enough the need for support in all areas of business. It is impossible that you know everything (even though sometimes you might think so), so it is imperative you surround yourself with a good team internally and broad range of support externally. Why do you think the President of the United States has a cabinet? No matter who the President is, he can't be an expert on everything in government and in the lives of the citizens he serves. He surrounds himself with experts who can advise him, then exercises the skill needed to take the information given him and make appropriate decisions.

The same is true in business. If you have your own law firm but are lousy with numbers, you'd better get a bookkeeper on the payroll. If you are a business owner on Main Street and your numbers are slowing, it is helpful to belong to a group of your neighboring merchants who can tell you why their numbers are rising, and give you solid advice to help yours do the same. My manager, Courtney W., at Beanstalks was a master of organization, much better at it than I was. She was a lot like Jim in this way. Either of them would make the *Container Store* look like a mess! We had a supply room in the lower level of Beanstalks, which was the heart of our operations. We managed sometimes up to a dozen parties at once, each with their own theme, decorations and favors, in many different quantities depending on the number of guests invited. These were in addition to our regular inventory, the utility closet, food storage and helium tank and balloon assortment that were also stored in the same space. Toward the back of the room, under the stairs was a miniscule amount of space with some shelving. Jim managed to store an entire Santa's Village back there, which included at least ten Christmas trees and a lit archway. I don't even want to think about what that room would have looked like if I had been in charge of keeping it together. I learned to take cues from both of them when it came to keeping things orderly.

Similarly, two of my day shift employees, Pat and Marge, were retirees with a lifetime of experience to learn from. They both had a tireless work ethic and were very knowledgeable. One taught me how to be more assertive when it was needed, whether it be to an advertiser on the phone or someone misusing our facility. The other had spent a lifetime in the restaurant business with her husband and was an ace at cutting costs when it came to food servings and equipment, as well as tips to make the health inspector happy. When you are building your empire, check your ego at the door. A good business person knows to keep learning, stay curious and ask questions. Learn from your successors, but stay open to new ideas from people you wouldn't ordinarily expect to get advice from, and build relationships with people you can help. In return they will help you.

Take Action TODAY

(20 minutes each)

1. Make a list of ways to stay involved with clients or colleagues in between projects/jobs. What other ways can you connect with them?
2. Pitch your new business ideas to people you know will be supportive and spread the word. Take their response under advisement. Have they thought of something you haven't?
3. Look through your contacts to see who has connections beneficial

to your endeavors? How can you help them in return? Make calls and set up meetings to discuss your plans.

4. Read your affirmation from Step One and stay confident.

Off Season Contact Form

Name of client/customer:______________________________

____

How often do I deal directly with this person?__________

____

When do I interact with them? *(weekly/monthly/summers)*_

____

____

How can I contact them during other times?___________

____

____

____

____

Name of client/customer:______________________________

____

How often do I deal directly with this person?__________

____

When do I interact with them? *(weekly/monthly/summers)*

____

____

How can I contact them during other times?____________

____

____

____

____

Practical Advice

There are two huge no-no's when it comes to networking. The first thing you can do to hinder a new or existing business relationship is to rush your pitch. This happens at networking events all the time I've done it too. Business relationships are all about trust. There is no way to trust a complete stranger who approaches you at a networking event with a thirty second pitch. You have nothing to go on other than this first impression, which for the moment is "pushy".

I love an article I read on smallbiztrends.com by Diane Helbig. She says, "People who pitch early don't understand the relationship building aspect of networking. They believe that simply participating in the activity is a license to sell. Well it isn't." In addition to early pitching, she also cautions against adding people to your email list without permission and assuming a closeness that isn't there. Adding someone to your list just because you have their business card is just plain rude. My readers are on my list because either they asked to be or commented they like what I write. If indeed I have someone on the list by mistake who asks to be removed (this happens), it is important to respond immediately and with an apology for any inconvenience I may have caused. Sometimes a respectful withdrawal makes a positive impact on its own, with an unexpected result.

People want to get to know you a little bit before agreeing to talk business. I read an article about a recording studio owner who was at a networking event. She found herself mingling with one of the largest music producers in the industry. Do you think she walked up to the producer, introduced herself and then started pitching her studio? No way. She struck up a conversation about the party they were at, about the hosts of the event, band, the food, whatever. You see it was a given that everyone in attendance was in the music industry. It was half way through dinner before the topic of her studio came up, and probably by someone else across the table. Then the studio owner had the opportunity to pitch her place and not come across as a hard seller, or someone desperate for business. This resulted in the producer asking the questions, drawing out all of the information and more that the studio head wanted to bring into the discussion in the first place. This doesn't mean you always have to tip toe around pitching your idea, but at a networking event, *everyone is there to sell,* so it is the method in which you do it that makes the difference.

Secondly, and this is by far the worst thing you could possibly do, is to openly bad mouth those around you to other colleagues, whether they be a neighboring business owner, a potential customer or a community organization. I remember one time I was hosting a booth for one of the organizations I am involved with. There were two of us, myself and a gentleman who had just launched his business. The gentleman didn't know much about me, or in particular what business organizations I was a part of. By the time the hour was up he had bent my ear continuously, verbally butchering one of the very organizations for which I was a Director. Not only did he have poor things to say about the organization, but he personally attacked several of our members. He was obnoxious, at best, and I for one was certain he was someone I would never consider giving my business to or doing business with. Even if he had been knocking something completely removed from myself, I just don't like to be around those kinds of bad manners. This guy was a freight train of negativity. I imagine this was the way he conducted all of his networking opportunities. Not surprisingly, his business didn't last.

Feed Your Energy

In addition to experts, you need people around you who offer emotional support. Surround yourself with people who share your passion. Find professional groups, online networks and organizations where you can turn to for support when things get nutty. Places I go as a writer include SheWrites.com, which is the equivalent of Facebook but is limited to female writers and authors. Speaking of Facebook, my writing page is probably the best place to hang out when I'm looking for emotional support. There I find my readers and have a direct line to people who like what I'm doing, and believe in my craft. I'm also a member of SCBWI, or the Society of Children's Book Writers and Illustrators, and I am a Chamber member and know that if I need business advice I can find someone to help. None of these, of course, take the place of a solid foundation of support at home. I'm lucky to have a family who cheers me on constantly, or is a sounding board for my frustration (James). It's not impossible to fight a wall toward forward motion if that is what you experience at home, but it sure makes life a lot easier.

Spin It: Turning Negative to Positive

So you've got your new idea, have your future picture playing in your head and are beginning to build business relationships. Good for you! You are on your way to where you want to be. That is, until you are sitting at your good friend's house, having a glass of wine, telling her all about your new business idea and how you are so excited. As a good friend will, she sits there riveted by your news, with eyes wide, sharing your enthusiasm, but her brother in law, visiting from

Paduca, overhears from another room and chimes in. "You actually think that is going to work?" followed by, "well I'm no business man but I *am* a consumer and I would NEVER go into a place like that!" Your first response is going to be to turn into a defensive linebacker and sack the guy. However, a more reasonable approach may be to pick his brain a little. Why wouldn't he visit your place of business? If it is offensive to him, why is that? Instead of defending what you already know is a fabulous, life changing business plan; use this negative Ned to tweak something you might not have thought of. Without even trying you've found yourself a willing participant in a focus group...and you don't even have to offer him refreshments or participation compensation. Clearly, however, it goes without saying you only spend time on people who are respectable, not abusive. There is a difference between listening to sound opinion and taking abuse from an arrogant nobody.

Not everyone is going to be a fan. Don't stick your head in the sand or let that queasy stomach kick in. Smile and say, "I'd love to hear why you feel that way!" and use what you learn. Just like obstacles are stepping stones, people can be the tour guides walking you up the steps.

BONUS Section: Mentors

There is no way I can write a chapter on Networking and not mention mentors. I know we've touched on them briefly in some of the action steps to help you find a mentor, but I want to take a minute to explain how invaluable they are when you find a good one. A mentor is a person who shares their knowledge in a field of expertise, to an up and comer who otherwise might not get it. There are two people I turn to in matters of business, whether I have specific questions or just need a shove in the right direction. It's not like I call them every week, but I could if I needed to and they would help me no matter what. One is a man named David R. I first met David in amongst other community members, as our paths crossed every so often in meetings or events. I really got to know him later, when I attended the Saline Leadership Institute, an organization for which he is a facilitator. Truly, the topics we covered at SLI were perfect catapults for asking good questions of the facilitators, but I just think David knows something about everything and a ton about many other things. When I needed help designing promotional materials, not only did he look over the postcards I was proposing, but he taught me what worked and explained why. When I wasn't sure how to get momentum for my writing business or the best way to find new clients, he met with me then too, pointing out my strengths as well as things I could do better. He has given me work and sent clients my way. He is a visionary and a brain- stormer and a business man who knows how to get things accomplished, but then takes great joy in passing along information to anyone who needs it. That is the difference between a mentor and a colleague. A mentor is always available, and *teaches* rather than *tells*.

My other mentor probably doesn't even know he is my mentor! His name is Art T. and he is what I like to call my community mentor. He's the guy who knows everyone in town, and has his finger on the pulse of everything happening in and around us at any moment, mostly because he's involved just about everywhere you look. He's a speaker, an organizer and get this, he *always* answers his phone! When it comes to staying involved in areas of community, which I mentioned earlier as a key factor in staying visible, Art is the master. He is the guy I call for anything involving community relations. I find his most valuable skill to be his ability to communicate with many different types of people, all with different personalities. He relates to anyone, and that isn't an easy skill to develop. I remember having lunch with him one day, when I was struggling with a decision regarding my community involvement. He knew exactly where my talents could be of best use, and where I could learn the most from my surroundings. Again, he teaches what he knows, and advises freely to those interested in learning. That is the true definition of a mentor.

Having a mentor or two is the grown-up, business equivalent to being in the Big Brothers/Big Sisters Clubs, and gives an entrepreneur, or even a seasoned business person a safety net of sorts, to call on when needed. Mentors deserve our appreciation and respect and reciprocation too, when we are in a position to provide it. I look forward to the day when I will be mentoring someone too!

Step Seven: Networking Summary

- Stay visible in between jobs, keep up relationships.
- Learn the skills of communication.
- Nobody can fly solo and succeed, surround yourself with experts.
- Look for connections in contact lists, set up meetings.
- Remember what not to do when networking, don't pitch too early or add people to e-mail lists without permission.
- Find emotional support to balance out professional support.
- When people don't like your idea, find out why and use that information.

April's Upwords # 9

There is no room for negativity anywhere or at anytime. Don't let it crowd you.

Step Eight: Platform

My Experience

As I've mentioned before, in my future picture I am writing, signing, speaking and motivating. Back when I started, I knew if I was going to be successful at any of those things, people had to recognize my name, and know the quality of my work. I had a pretty good start locally, as people knew me from Beanstalks and they started seeing my byline in the local paper week after week. But that was only in my home town. I knew I had to have a broader reach. I started writing for bigger, further reaching newspapers and created my own blog. There were different things I wanted to write about, each having their own *feel* or range of topics. Eventually, recognizing that some different topics might interest different people, one blog turned into five. In order to get those read, I made arrangements for bigger publications to link to them, or "pick them up". I was able to do this in exchange for posting a widget, used as an advertising link, of the publication linking to my blog. Suddenly, I had access to thousands of readers. Of course, this didn't mean that everyone who saw my link clicked on it and read my work, but a certain percentage did. Finally, comments on my blogs started coming in from all over the world. I had so many from different locations across the globe, my husband decided to start tracking my readers on a map. It was no time at all before I had readers on five continents. Now that was the reach I was looking for!

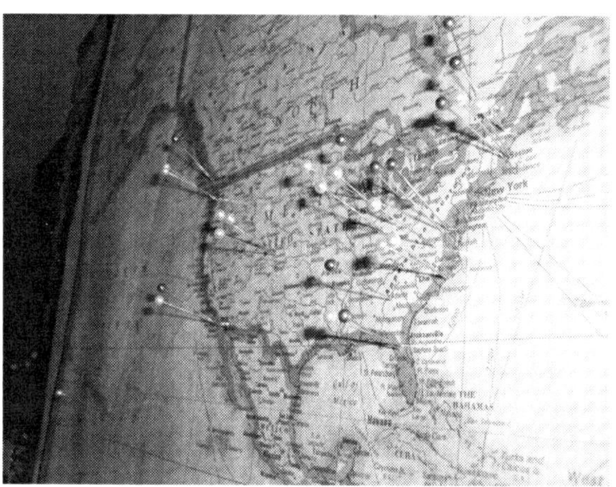

My map of readers in my first few months of writing.

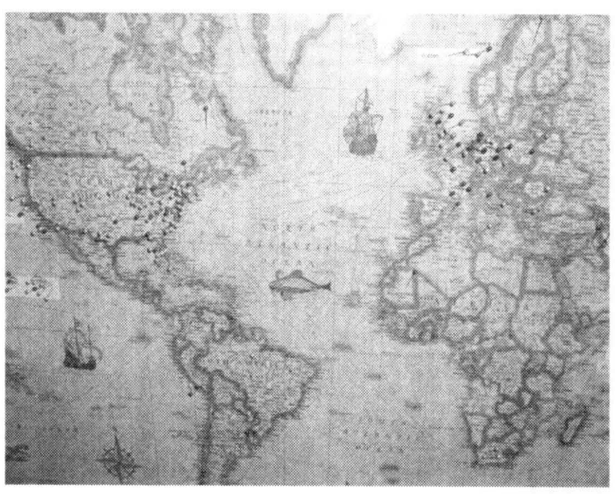

Readers across Europe, South America and Africa within one year of writing.

The more I wrote the more exposure I got. I did a radio interview, and was featured in a Passions and Pursuits section of the newspaper. Suddenly, people were taking notice of my writing. Another contact led to my internet television projects. Turns out, A2YP.TV (now WDEE.TV) was looking for a female sports commentator. My blog "Sports For Chicks" was proof I knew my stuff and would qualify me for that position. Then, when A2YP.TV needed a host for their business show, "The Business Spotlight", things just fell into place with that project and the publishing of this book falling hand in hand.

Call it the trickledown effect, or being in the right place at the right time if you like. I call it working my butt off to be seen and heard. Most of what I wrote my first year after Beanstalks closed was as a contributor, which means I didn't get paid for any of it. As tough as that was in the beginning, the exposure I got for it was priceless. Today, if you search my name on the web, you will find at least three full pages of links to my writing and my public community involvement. I was making a name for myself and building a quality reputation. This was the foundation of my platform, which grows bigger and broader each day now, with every word that I type.

Stats and Stuff You Need to Know

So what is a platform anyway? A platform is your personal brand. It is a means of publicity and professional celebrity for anyone trying to be more visible in their field. The cool thing is it works for *anyone* in *any field*, not just writers, performers or politicians. For example, let's go back to the plumbing company owner mentioned in an earlier chapter. A platform for him will create a status of expertise. He will join professional unions and organizations for his trade. He will comment or send articles to various plumbing trade publications. He will set up a blog on his website with plumbing tips and how-to videos, as well as uploading those videos to other venues like YouTube. When there is a plumbing disaster, like a busted pipe or major flooding, he will offer his assistance. He will stay current on the latest plumbing technology and maintain stellar customer service. All of these scenarios up his expertise and exposure. People start to take notice. Before he knows it he is being called to speak to those same trade organizations, he is being quoted in trade magazines and other sorts of media. His new platform builds consumer confidence in his company. And there you have it, a rock star in the plumbing industry, which not only boosts exposure; it doubles or triples his income.

I have to recommend a book on personal branding. I've read it three or four times and refer back to it regularly. It is Fame 101 by Jay and Maggie Jessup. I highly recommend you get this book, about how to get famous, if you want to get beyond your cubicle, office or dining room table. Good businesses succeed because of exposure. Anyone can seek and buy advertising for their company, but advertise the woman/man at the helm of the company and suddenly the advertising comes to you, bringing with it opportunity after opportunity.

The Jessups talk about building your personal brand as a business unto yourself. They say, "Great personal branding is the difference between being the vice president of product development at a company and being "that 'hot new creative guy we've got on a two year contract.' Same position, same person -- quadruple the perceived value and likely quadruple the compensation."

Building a platform is about creating success above and beyond your industry and monetizing your expertise. Can you have success without a platform? Of course. But if it is your name and face at the helm of your business, why wouldn't you want to do everything in your power to bring more success to your company? You might be one of those people who opened up a business from the heart, with the sole purpose of fulfilling your life's dream and giving back to your community. That's great. But think of how much more you can give back if you are a more visible expert in your field. Good media exposure brings you credibility that leads to more customers, more money to give, and a greater audience for your cause. For example, let's say you have a shoe shop and you are known within your little community as a business that always helps out local events and sponsors home town little league teams. Your truest passion however, is raising awareness and helping to research the causes and cure of children's orthopedic disorders. You are so passionate about it, that half of your inventory is in orthotic shoes for these special customers. You do a sound business and even bring in customers within a fifteen mile radius, both because of the quality of your product and the convenience of your location. The locals already know about you so you have some name recognition and reputation to build on. Now, how would taking your platform a step further be beneficial? What if you were to call up the American Pediatric Association and tell them about your shoes, and fundraising possibilities? Not only would a joint project put you on their national map, but suddenly you have an event to take to local media. Let your local newspapers pump up your nationally endorsed cause. Call local radio and television stations, show them your shoes and ask them to feature your event. Send press releases to running, fitness and medical publications to let them know your special orthotic shoes are getting national attention, and if they get involved promoting your fundraiser, they in turn, get exposure too. Before you know it, you are an expert on orthotic shoes and have to come up with a way to do mail order business because you have people all over the country who want your shoes! You say you are not in business for the money (not even a little?), then instead of thinking about how much of a profit you are going to pocket, think about how big of a check you can hand over to the American Pediatric Association, and you might even be able to sponsor the entire Little League, instead of just a team or two.

Why This Step (Platform) Is So Important

Leaving profitability aside, visibility gives you credibility. If the public and media outlets are citing you as an expert, how does that make your business look? Credibility, dependability and respect are the components of a business's foundation that give it staying power, longevity. A good platform will help your company be one people look back on decades from now. These are the kinds of businesses we hear about for years, where families pass down their values of intimate customer service and reputation of stellar quality. It's like the jewelry store on the corner that has been in the same building with the same red velvet lined window casings. Everyone knows it has been there since 1940-something, that it is the *only* place to go for quality diamonds, and that the family has been a staple of the community for generations. The head buyer is the great, great nephew of the company founder, and at least one of his kids will likely keep the family business going. Their family name is on every guest list of every major event, and their expertise is sought industry - wide.

Everyone recognizes the family portrait, and can put a face with the name that still hangs over the marble entryway. This is longevity brought about by credibility, brought about by visibility, brought about by platform.

Take Action TODAY

(twenty minutes to an hour each)

1. Google yourself. How much information is there in cyberspace about your professional endeavors? If not at least three pages, you need to start focusing on building your web presence.
2. If you don't have a website, get one immediately. Consumers expect you to be on the web. There are lots of companies who host websites and keep them simple to create.
3. Read Jay and Maggie Jessup's book Fame 101.
4. Take advantage of Social Networking; get business profiles on every network you can think of.

Visibility Worksheet

Write down five ways you can make yourself and your business more visible in the next thirty days:

Start Date:________________

1. ____

2. ____

3. ____

4. ____

5. ____

Goal date *(thirty days from start date)*:___________________

Practical Advice

Some of you may be in a position to hire a Public Relations firm to help you with your brand, be it personal, professional or both. PR agents can indeed get you exposure at sometimes lightening speeds, but you have to be in a position to afford them. Good agents are expensive, with smaller agencies asking anywhere between $2,000 and $5,000 per month retainer, and then adding on as actions permit. Due to the high fees, there is a lot of controversy among different companies and professionals as to whether or not hiring a public relations professional is worth the time, effort and money. Margaret Heffernan wrote an article earlier this year for BNET where she stated twice having paid large sums for no results. Heffernan says, "What did we get for $5000? Nothing. A few glossy presentations that echoed back what we already knew. Some press releases. But that was it." Some businesses are just too small for the bigger firms to really pay attention to, and with smaller firms sometimes they lack the experience or credibility to land any substantial publicity.

An article by Microsoft writer Joanna L. Krotz encourages us all to not get discouraged, that there is a method to the madness of securing a good firm. First and foremost is doing your homework and finding an agent who understands what it is you do and who you are. A giant firm who has never heard of your product is going to have to charge you research hours to understand your target audience. A smaller firm, who specializes in your field of expertise, would be a better way to go.

When it comes to paying out the big bucks, be upfront with your budget. Let them know you have X amount of dollars and are firm. Then, let them map out a plan that works within the numbers you have submitted. Stay close to your project by asking for regular progress reports and decide what it is going to take for you to feel successful. Perhaps success for your business isn't how many radio interviews you get, but is better measured by the amount of new customers on your contact list. And lastly, what should be obvious to any public relations agent, publicist, media specialist, analyst or communications specialist, is they must be absolutely current on technology, the web and social networking. The days of a single press release are long gone.

Feed Your Energy

I'm going to be blunt here. Don't get a big head. Nobody wants to book an arrogant personality on their show, nor are they going to go out of their way to write you a complimentary article. This is especially true in journalism, as a true reporter is schooled to write "just the facts, ma'am," so if you are a jerk, you will be portrayed as one. It is just as important to treat the press with respect as it is your colleagues and clients. Do you want a radio personality to refer you to a newspaper or television contact they have? Do you want them to continue to talk about you and your product long after you've left the studio? Make sure you leave a good impression. Remember when I talked about "give, give, give" and not "take, take, take"? This is another instance where this rule of thumb is pertinent. A television appearance, radio interview or any other media exposure is not about you, it is about your audience. You are giving them what they want, a way to get a little bit closer to you or your product. It's not about inflating your ego.

Spin It: Turning Negative to Positive

What is it they say? Bad press is still press? True, and in some cases a headline stays in the limelight a heck of a lot longer if there is a scandal involved. Only you can decide if this is the way you want to go. We hear about PR stunts all of the time in politics and Hollywood. Look at Howard Stern for instance. It would be difficult to find someone more controversial, yet he is one shock jock who is banking on bad publicity. His nasty news is what makes him the highest paid disc jockey in the country.

During an election year, we are exposed to hours of negative campaign ads. Billions of dollars are spent on candidates nationwide out to ruin the reputations of their opponents. Does it work? Sure it does. Negative publicity is still publicity. It's like when you have a terrible experience at a department store, where you are treated rudely by a cashier. Are you more likely to tell people about your bad experience than if you had had a routine shopping trip with nothing to report? According to studies, you will tell nine people about the negative experience for every one person you tell about a positive experience.

So what do you do when you are the victim of a smear ad? Or a false statement is made about your product? First and foremost assess the statement being made and decide if it is true or not. If it is, acknowledge it, apologize and fix it. If it isn't true, then get you or your spin doctors out on the denial trail with facts in place to dispute all evidence to the contrary. And of course, seek legal advice immediately.

Step Eight: Platform Summary

- Remember my story, one bit of publicity leads to another and another, get your name out there.
- Platform is your personal brand.
- Visibility is credibility.
- Google yourself, have a web presence, read books on personal branding.
- Do your homework to decide if a PR firm is for you.
- Don't get a big head.
- Bad press is still press, decide if it is for you.
- Assess any accusations or bad press put upon you by others, then deal with them appropriately.

April's Upwords # 29

You are invincible. You know what you want so go and get it already!

Step Nine: Image

My Experience

As much as I absolutely love that I work from my home office and can wear my comfy clothes and moose slippers while I work, there is no way (until this book is published!) any of my clients or readers would know it. The minute I walk out the door for a meeting, a taping or to attend an event, it's all business from my hair down to my heels.

In my day to day life, I play different roles. I am a mom at home (moose slippers), PTA and football mom (casual and conservative), a business woman (professional), an internet television personality (professional +), and a writer (business to business casual). In addition, the community role I play might have me attending an evening event requiring more formal attire. And this still doesn't count a date night with my husband or a girl's night out on the town. I'm not telling you this so you'll think I have a closet the size of New Hampshire, I'm just making a point that the key to a successful impression is to present myself appropriately, depending on the occasion.

As much as I don't like to admit it, image does matter. The way we look, or are looked upon, makes a huge difference in whether doors open for us, or not. It's not about fitting into stereotypes or trying to look like magazine cover models (thank goodness), it is about looking the absolute best that we can. I know when I am crisp and professional, I feel more confident, and that confidence carries into my board meeting. I know if I take care of myself and attend to my appearance, then my client will believe I'll attend to my work just as well. It's not about being a diva, or being beautiful. It's about being neat, clean and appropriate.

I'll never forget the panic I felt, even if just for a few minutes, the day I was told the internet television show I was hosting was for a *minimum* of thirteen episodes. Thirteen episodes! I didn't have that many outfits and there was no way I was going to get caught wearing the same thing twice on TV. I mean really, you don't see Oprah or Ellen or even Montel Williams wearing the same thing twice! I however, am not on Oprah's budget. Eventually, I would get a wardrobe sponsor, but in the beginning I was freaking out trying to figure out how I was going to "look the part" thirteen different times. Well, there are ways around my dilemma and I just had to get creative, and do it with what I could afford. I learned to really mix and match, to leave my ego and shop consignment, discount and even Goodwill (yep!). Resale and discount stores were a great resource, as long as I found things that were current, and if they weren't current, they had to be retro enough to become current with the right accessories. I shopped clearance sales in high end stores. Yes, there are places to get $350 business suits for under $100. Once again, obstacles become stepping stones, it is all in how you see them.

Other image issues are personal hygiene (should be a no brainer), a good hair cut and/or color and good posture. Top that off with intelligent communication skills and a firm handshake, eye contact and TA-DA, the makings of an appropriately grand first impression.

This would be a good point to talk about cell phones as well. Ladies, cell phones are not fashion accessories, they are business accessories. Cell phone etiquette can have as much of an impact on your image as your way-too-dangly earrings. Step away from the cell phone. Newsflash: You are not invisible when you are staring at your phone. People notice. Your children, your husband, anybody you are supposed to be looking in the eye, they all see you *ignoring them*. Before you tell me "oh, that's not true April, I can pay attention to what is going on and still text or check my e-mail", just stop. Everyone in attendance at the board meeting sees the one member not engaged in the discussion at hand, but heavily engaged to his/her Blackberry. I'm sure you think you can successfully multi-task. I was sure I could too, until my youngest son just stopped talking mid-sentence and walked out of the room. As far as he was concerned, my phone/e-mail was more important than he was. It has never happened since. It seems silly to even have to mention that no e-mail, text or phone call is ever as important as a member of your family or support team, or that perhaps you should be tuning in to the vote that just happened during your board meeting. Put down your phones Superwomen. You can't do it all, all of the time.

Stats and Stuff You Need to Know

One of my favorite daily e-mails into my inbox is from Pink Magazine (P.inc.). It is a business magazine for women and is chock full of all things useful for women working in all different fields. They have a daily blog called "Little Pink Book", and one post earlier this month caught my attention. It was about dressing for success on the job, and in this case it mentioned dressing for one job level above the position you are in. Now doesn't that just scream FUTURE PICTURE? Remember back in Step One when we were talking about mindset, and how it is beneficial to act as if you already have what it is you are after? Even I hadn't thought of it in terms of wardrobe but it made perfect sense to me when I read it. The other point this particular post made that I really liked was how you dress not only shows self-respect, but it shows respect toward your client. Think about other times you dress out of respect. Some people dress in their "Sunday best" for church as respect to their God, we dress up for weddings and funerals out of respect for the bride and groom or the family of the deceased. We wear football jerseys and paint our faces out of respect for our favorite teams and players, or find just the right outfit out of respect for a suitor on a first date. Why should it be any different in a business environment?

If you are feeling a little intimidated by all of this fashionista talk, don't. I am no fashionista and I'm doing just fine. There are basic rules that are easy to follow. Many fashion guides are available to help, especially if you check out all of the job finder, career builder type websites and magazines. First, even though sex sells in advertising, when it comes to business, keep things covered if you want to be taken seriously. Second, dress your age. 40 and 50 somethings shouldn't be caught dead in a store that caters to 20 somethings. Sometimes women think dressing younger will turn back the clock. Not so much. In fact, you're more likely aging yourself and even looking a little desperate for yesteryear. More mature women have many youthful, current fashion options in today's market. Don't sell yourself short, forty is the new twenty after all, and we all can look, feel and be amazing! The same goes for dressing older than you need to. Don't get too frumpy too soon, you'll appear dated and not at all clued in to whatever market or business you are in.

If you still aren't sure how you are supposed to carry yourself, take a look around at other people you look up to, or those similar to your age who are successful in their fields. Without being a stalker, study what they wear, how they look, their posture and facial expressions. What is the sincerest form of flattery? You guessed it, imitation!

Why This Step (Image) Is So Important

No matter how skilled you are, how much expertise you have, who you've been trained by or how many degrees you hold, you won't get a chance of putting any of it to use if you can't get past the front door. Opportunities in business and life are everywhere, and often are spontaneous. You must be ready at any time. A first impression is the key to getting that door open, and then your skill set and talent will keep the doors coming. Here is an example.

When I met Tony Dixon, CEO of WDEE.TV, it wasn't because I was seeking work. I was filling in for our local Chamber's executive director on the weekly radio broadcast (WLBY in Ann Arbor with Lucy Ann Lance) about our local Chamber events. Often in these on-air appearances, we invite our members to join us to promote their businesses. WDEE.TV was a new member, so I invited Tony along to talk about his new and exciting internet television network. I had never met Tony before. I wasn't looking to get any business out of this appearance. We were there to promote Tony's business, not mine, and we were going to be on the radio, not in front of a live audience. Did I have to get dressed for success? Not really. Did I anyway? You bet I did.

While Tony and I were sitting in the lobby waiting for our turn on-air, we started talking football. He was looking for a female sports commentator and I happen to know a thing or two about sports. The ten minutes in the lobby turned into an interview of sorts to see if I knew my stuff. He asked technical questions and asked my opinion of certain players. I was sure to throw in current information about other teams and players' scandals that were happening at the time, and we talked penalties and plays and rookies. Right before we were called to the studio, Tony said, "You *do* know football." By the time the interview was over, we were headed to the nearest coffee shop to talk business. He was looking for a sports chick, and I was it. Now, I wonder if that first football question would have even come out of his mouth if I hadn't looked professional? Remember, he needed someone to be on camera. Think of the opportunity I may have missed if I hadn't been dressed appropriately or carried myself with confidence. One door led to another, and now in addition to my sports blog being linked to his site, I'm the host of WDEE's business show, *The Business Spotlight*.

Take Action TODAY

(20 minutes each)

1. Thumb through some fashion and business magazines to get ideas about how you should present yourself at work, given the type of business you are in

2. Pay for a good, current haircut.
3. Practice good posture. If you sit at a desk a lot like I do, try switching out your office chair occasionally for a stability ball
4. Practice enunciating your words with the cork exercise (see end of this chapter)

Image Booster

Use these questions to help sharpen your Image

Name three people whose style you admire:

____

____

____

What is it about their style that you like? ____________

____

____

____

How can you implement some of their style into your image?

____

____

____

What do you consider your strong points in regards to your image?

____

____

____

What are your not-so-strong points?______________

____

____

____

What can you do to boost your confidence in these areas?

____

____

____

Practical Advice

We've spent a lot of time in this chapter talking about outward appearance. Do you know you can look like a million bucks and be a Rhodes Scholar, but if the minute you open your mouth you sound like a school girl on helium or your uncle Carl after sixty years of smoking non-filtered cigarettes, you can consider almost any opportunity lost?

According to voice coach specialist and vocal expert Marlena Reigh of YourVoiceSuceess.com, "You only have seconds to project a voice quality that has others deciding whether to listen to you, trust you or do business with you." Seconds. That is the same amount of time someone may spend taking a first glance at your appearance. How about if you are on the telephone? You have seconds before the person on the other end forms a mental picture in their mind. What does the mental picture of you look like when you speak on the phone? The way we sound when we speak says a ton about us. We can tell whether or not a person is confident, knowledgeable or high strung just by the way they introduce themselves.

I attended a two-part seminar that Marlena was teaching locally, and was extremely energized by her enthusiasm. What stood out for me is the fact that the energy behind the voice is as important as the voice quality itself (this works hand in hand with Mindset-Step One). You may have a smooth, musical voice that is very pleasant to listen to, but if you aren't engaged, committed and enthused about the content you are speaking of, your listeners are going to tune out. According to Marlena, there are voice techniques to "keep your audience interested, motivated to action, and left remembering what was said to the point of telling other people." She teaches the importance of using your breath, volume, rate, pitch, articulation and voice quality (how pleasing your voice is to listen to), and "HOW you say something, not what you say, leaves a lasting impression." Thanks to Marlena Reigh, I know improving my voice will give me confidence, make me a better listener and keep people interested in what I have to say. She says, "The sound of your voice can be seven times more important than what you say." Simply put, voice matters. Don't ignore it.

Feed Your Energy

Image is a tough one, I know. We all have things about ourselves, especially our physical appearance that makes us feel like the awkward adolescent we were in middle school. As difficult as it may seem, you've got to get over it. Unfortunately, appearance does matter in business. Ugh. I hate even saying it but it is true.

One could argue, *I could argue*, that success is measured in different ways, not necessarily only if you are in the top floor, corner office with a view, wearing Prada and power pumps. Success is personal to each individual and if you are in a job or have a company where you perform optimally not having to worry about your appearance, good for you! For the rest of us, just do what I do. Growl for a minute, then fit your workout in. I ask again, how bad do you want what you are after?

Another hurdle you are going to have to deal with is the ridiculous double standard placed upon women in the workplace. Unfortunately, if we look too good or sexy, it is assumed we have no brain. If we are too conservative with zero sex appeal, we don't have the same chances of getting hired as a woman who does. It is total insanity but certainly happens in the real world. Because we are smart, capable and strong, we assert a kind of power in the workplace. It is really a catch-22. If we look frumpy we don't get hired. If we are attractive, we must be stupid. If we assert any kind of power, we are either hired for that power or skipped over because it makes the boss uncomfortable. There are many different scenarios and no one formula for handling them. You stand the best chance in a room if you know your stuff, behave professionally and exude confidence.

Spin It: Turning Negative to Positive

For some, one problem of having a great image may be finding the money to look good. You think I own a Prada suit? Not yet, but I will. I mentioned earlier shopping at Goodwill. Don't you dare walk into that store hanging your head. This is a temporary situation, a necessary step to the next great thing. First, be grateful someone with a designer label discarded something for you to wear. Second, think of the good you are doing, knowing the money you are spending on somebody's hand me down, is going to a great charity. Remember, it is not always about you. There is a bigger picture. Stay grounded.

Step Nine: Image Summary

- Remember my story; you play different roles in your everyday lives, look appropriate.
- Dress for the job position one level up, respect your client/customers with the way you look.
- If you are lost when it comes to fashion, check out magazines or look at other leaders in their fields.
- First impressions are the difference between getting through that open door to showcase your qualifications, or not.
- Get a good hair cut.
- Your voice and how you speak is as important as how you look and what you know (www.YourVoiceSuccess.com).
- Appearance matters, unfortunate but true.
- There is nothing shameful in shopping at discount stores and charities. It's not forever.

Special Project: Enunciation Exercise

When I was a student at the American Academy of Dramatic Arts, I was in a Speech and Movement Class. One of the exercises we were taught to help us with enunciation and articulation was with the use of a cork.

What you'll need: one cork, any wine bottle will do. If you don't drink wine, borrow one or use something of similar size and shape.

What to do: Place the cork in between your front top and bottom teeth, and talk with it there. Note: Please be careful, corks are "chokables" so use common sense. Make sure you move your mouth and lips around the cork and speak as clearly as you possibly can. I know this feels funny but it works great. I used to have to recite Shakespeare for my Speech class. I would practice the speech over and over again with the cork in my mouth, but especially right before I was to perform it. You will be amazed how the muscles in your face automatically move with ease, once the cork is out, and enunciate every vowel and consonant with perfect precision. Try it next time you're pitching your idea or speaking at a function. I think you'll be as amazed as I was!

April's Upwords #12

Surround yourself with people who lift you up, to keep you just out of reach from anyone wanting to bring you down.

Step Ten: Support Systems

My Experience

I've talked throughout the book about keeping it real, staying grounded, not getting a big head and any other pompous cliché you'd like to insert here, but most importantly how "it's not always about you." However, during this crazy time of recovering from one business or starting the next, it does help to have one or more supportive people orbiting around you. I was lucky. Not everyone has the support system at home that I do. When I was on the couch for three weeks, my husband kept the rest of our world in motion. He took care of dinners, cleaned up the house, kept our boys on schedule, all while managing his own job, clearing out Beanstalks and shoveling record snowfall for that particular winter. My teenager cracked me up like only he can. My favorite is when I correct him on something minor, like leaving his shoes in the doorway, and him acting like I just called him a criminal, "geez mom, thanks a lot, I didn't mean tooooooo" in as sorrowful a voice as he can muster up. And then there is my little guy who hugged me one broken piece at a time, and even offered to let me sleep with his stuffed cat. I didn't get blamed, I just got consoled and encouraged.

Today, I know if I'm on a roll writing I can count on them not to interrupt me unless it is really important (like a missing Lego piece or something-ha!). Or if it is getting late and I still have much to do, I'll hear the coffee grinder upstairs in the kitchen and know there is a fresh pot being made just for me. All of my published work is celebrated, even if it is only a two-inch mention of a local PTA Carnival. They, my boys, are always behind me.

I do realize there are some women who aren't so lucky. They have spouses who don't want them to take the plunge, or don't think them capable, or at the very least don't even try to offer support. One woman I know wanted to take night classes to further her education, but her husband wouldn't give up playing hockey once a week to help out with the kids. Another woman I know does all of her business planning behind her husband's back because she knows he doesn't approve. For another woman, it is her parents who do not approve of her trying to start her own business. They want her to get a "real job" and stop daydreaming. Just so you know, this kind of behavior makes me nuts, but being angry about it certainly doesn't help these strong and capable, entrepreneurial women. I feel it is important for me to make a point here. There is a difference between having someone not support you and having someone abuse you.

I'll never forget a family I crossed paths with many years ago. I think of them every now and again. I was in my early twenties, waiting tables at a family restaurant. A man came in with his wife (presumably) and child. When I arrived to take their order, I asked the lady first what she would like to have. She held her face down the entire time, and wouldn't look up at me. I could tell she had some scrapes and bruises and was immediately suspicious. The man spoke to me gruffly and said, "You will speak to me, not her. I will tell you what she is going to eat." I was so struck I wasn't sure how to respond. He gave me the order for all three of them. Later when I came back around with coffee, I automatically just asked, "Would you like more coffee ma'am?" What a mistake. She began to say "Yes please" and he cut her off saying to her, "Did I say you could speak to this waitress?" Well, I was twenty-something and fearless and furious, and didn't quite have a handle on my professional skills yet, so I let the guy have it. I told him I wouldn't listen to him anymore and would only engage in conversation with his wife. If he wanted something, he'd have to have *her* ask for it. Of course, he called for my manager. The guy was *so* vile. He wound up leaving me a penny for a tip, and called me a name or two on the way out. I was so infuriated I went out right after him and threw the penny in his direction. I'm sure I probably mentioned what I thought he could do with his penny! I wonder if that woman ever got away from that man. Again, I tell this story now, because I want to make it clear there is a difference between not being supported and being abused. If you are in a situation of the latter, I have included some safe alternatives for you that may be helpful in the resources section, found in the back of this book. If you aren't sure which category you fall in, perhaps these questions will help. I know this isn't a book about relationships, but this is a subject I care deeply about. In order to have personal success, we must respect ourselves. If we allow ourselves to be mistreated, success can't be achieved. Every one of us deserves what we dream of.

Relationship Support Assessment

1. **Is your partner jealous?**
2. **Does your partner keep you from seeing friends or family on your own?**
3. **Does your partner call you to see where you are, or constantly check in?**
4. **Does your partner call you negative names or swear at you?**
5. **Are you ever afraid of your partner?**
6. **Does your partner lose their temper with you often?**
7. **Does your partner take your money?**
8. **Is your partner super nice sometimes and really mean other times?**
9. **Has your partner ever called you stupid?**
10. **Does your partner ever abuse your kids or your pets?**

If you answered any of the above questions with a "yes", please talk with someone about your relationship.

It is tough sometimes to be at the top of your game. Some partners are going to be uncomfortable, threatened even, by your intelligence, capabilities and strengths. If this is unfamiliar territory, or if you don't feel naturally comfortable in this kind of a role, don't be afraid to ask for guidance, and refer back to Step 3.

Stats and Stuff You Need to Know

Support systems don't have to come in the form of a spouse and kids like mine do. Whoever it is in your life you recognize for guaranteed, genuine, lean-on-me-status-no-matter-what is the one to go to here. Perhaps it's your gal pals, your grandfather or a wise neighbor lady. Maybe you've only got your two golden retrievers and a fish. If they help you through triumph and heartache, then they'll work just fine. You must realize you have the power over your own life, but it's nice to have back up. In fact, it is important to note, that since the rise and fall of Beanstalks, I have learned about a different type of support for entrepreneurs.

Being an entrepreneur can be a very lonely job. Unless you are starting up with extra cash to hire a bunch of employees, you spend a lot of time isolated from the rest of the world while you are solving one problem after another trying to get your business going. Back when I was a start-up, I didn't know about groups like *Starve Ups* in Portland, or Emotional Intelligence groups being taught at business schools. I did have mentors and fellow business owners to ask for help, but didn't want to come across as too clueless. Turns out, there were groups of other "me's" out there all feeling the same way! Entrepreneurial support groups range from one other person (a mini-group) to about fifteen people. They are all in about the same stages of their start-up and can choose to meet up once per week, bi-monthly or as often as they choose. The members do not need to be in the same types of businesses, as most start-ups at their earliest stages are very similar, whether they are grape producers or software developers.

Starve Ups is a non-profit organization in the business of helping entrepreneurs in the very early stages of their businesses. They began with seven entrepreneurs as members back in 2000, and have now capped the number of members at twenty-two, so they can stay small and focused on the people and companies they choose to help. After ten years, 85% of their members are still in business, 65% of them are profitable with average annual revenue of $2.5 Million. These are terrific numbers! Whether you have the optimal emotional support at home like I did, or hang out alone with your dogs and your fish, you will benefit from an entrepreneurial emotional support group. If and when I am a start-up again, I will definitely seek this kind of group, and if there isn't one in my area, I'll start one. You can too!

Why This Step (Support Systems) Is So Important

I've said it throughout the book, going solo is only for patting yourself on the back, which is good, but better if you've got other people doing it too. You can't possibly know everything, and handle everything that presents itself when you are building a business. I am one of those women who believe we can have it all. We can balance work and family and whatever else we choose to pick up. But, there is a secret to this kind of success. I believe we can all be Superwomen, we just can't be Superwomen all of the time. We need breaks. We need help. We need support. Reaching out is a sign of strength, not weakness. It demonstrates we are smart enough to ask for help when it is needed. Even Wonder Woman had back -up.

Take Action TODAY

(twenty minutes to one hour per week)

1. Write down where you are struggling. Make a list of things you don't know, as well as what you do know.
2. Seek out an entrepreneurial support group. Have your list ready for the first meeting. Ask questions you need answered and offer up what you know is working.

In Need of Solutions: Use this worksheet to help nail down your obstacles so you can learn and turn them into stepping stones.

I am struggling with________________________________

____

____

____

Specifically, in regards to the above obstacle, I need to know

____

____

____

The best group/person to find a solution to this obstacle is

____

____

Date and time I am meeting with this group/person

____

I have learned the solution to this obstacle, it is

____

____

____

3. When your new business is taking time away from your kids or spouse, pick a time to let them help with something. There will be SOMETHING they can do, and they'll get to do it while spending time with you.

Practical Advice

Business support groups are such a great idea, that if you don't have one near you, you should start one. Here are some pointers on how to do that:

1. Visit County records to see who has registered a new business or DBA (doing business as). You can also check with business school message boards, or even put an ad in a business journal that says you are seeking fellow start-up business owners.
2. Set up meetings once a week (in the beginning) to chat and exchange notes, ideas, answer each other's questions.
3. Eventually, when you know areas in which you are all struggling, ask an expert in that area to speak at a meeting. There are lots of mentors and successful business owners who will do this for a cup of coffee. Use your contacts and networking groups we talked about in Step Seven. If you still don't know anyone, ask your local Chamber of Commerce for a good source. There is safety in numbers when it comes to asking people you don't know for help.

Feed Your Energy

Isolation is a risky business. Don't get swallowed up by your start-up. Believe it or not, there are hours in the day where you don't have to be on the phone or on site. This is especially important if you have family waiting in the wings cheering you on. They will cheer your idea, and support your efforts, but they will miss you too, and you will miss them. Nurture what you need to nurture to get through the day.

I hated being away from my kids. They were part of the reason I opened a business like Beanstalks, because I knew they could hang there with me when I was at work. But even then, I was *working* at work, and not really spending time with them. Contrary to popular belief, being your own boss, at least in the beginning, does not allow you more free time. It is just the opposite. When I was at the phone company, I was off work by 3:30 pm. With my own place I was lucky if I made it home by 7:00 pm and I worked on weekends! It became very important to us all that we find time to just *be* together.

You don't want your support system to resent your new endeavor, that is a sure way to put a glitch in the future picture. You don't want to feel guilty for not spending time with those who love you because guilt is the quickest way to cut into your productivity. You have to find a way to balance your work and your personal support system. They are there for you, so be sure and make time for them during your 70 hour work week. It's about prioritizing and keeping good energy around you. Negativity kills success.

Spin It- Turning Negative to Positive

The biggest obstacle here is not wanting to look stupid. Here you are, you've got a storefront, but aren't open yet. You must be doing something right because you are standing in a brick and mortar and your name is on the lease. The community is buzzing with anticipation of your opening. The bank is congratulating you on the approval of your business loan. The Chamber of Commerce has scheduled a ribbon cutting in your honor. Even the Mayor is coming! So how on earth are you going to tell everyone you may not be opening because you didn't know you had to have a sink installed just to sell coffee, and that you might not pass the health inspection in time to open if you don't get that sink installed? And then, turns out there is only a miniscule of space for the sink and it has to be special ordered to fit. Not to mention you're going to have to tell the carpenter who just completed your custom cabinetry that he has to tear it out to make room for a sink. Oh, and then there is this rule with the health department that says you have to have a drain anywhere you have a sink, which means you are calling the plumber back, and then the back splash has to be a material completely different than what you have just painted, and before you know it you've spent an additional $30,000 because you didn't call the health inspector "just to serve coffee." (ahem...this is a completely made up scenario...honest...)

You only *thought* it was a stupid question to ask a coffee shop up the street if they had a sink. You'd have looked a lot smarter if you'd asked. Didn't your teacher tell you? There is no such thing as a stupid question. *Use your support systems.* Take your lack of knowledge and spin it into an opportunity to learn something new, and in this case, a better way to spend $30,000.

Step Ten: Support Systems Summary

- Remember my story, support at home is irreplaceable, if you are lucky enough to have it, be thankful.
- If you don't have support at home, or even if you do, seek support from an entrepreneurial support group, someone in your shoes.
- Total isolation is non-productive.
- Start a support group of your own.
- Ask for help, there are no stupid questions.

April's Upwords # 20

Every day you make choices. You can make the ones that move you forward, or make the ones that take you back or leave you stuck. Onward already!

Step Eleven: Money

My experience

Money is the difference between keeping your dream/idea/business on paper or seeing it in the real or virtual world with doors you will walk through, or a website you will manage. When I was seeking funds for Beanstalks, I had six different banks tell me "no thanks" before I had one say "yes". Most banks asked me to drop off my business plan for their review, and told me they'd get back to me. Some took a week, some took two weeks. When they did call, I would get a standard verbalized version of a form letter stating, "We're sorry Mrs. Scarlett, this plan isn't for us but we wish you the best of luck in the future." Eventually I asked for more concrete reasons why I was being turned down. I reviewed the recommendations and made some changes, but those changes still didn't land me the "yes" I was looking for.

It was extremely frustrating. I remember slugging through the spring mud to work on cable at the phone company, literally trying to will my phone to ring. It didn't. I was running out of local banks. How could I be so sure about my idea, so passionate about its possibilities, and yet still be unfunded? It was obvious my enthusiasm wasn't leaping off the pages of the business plan so I decided the next bank would be different. When they asked me to drop off my business plan, I politely requested a fifteen minute meeting to discuss my plan before leaving it in the hands of the numbers people. It was at this meeting I was able to pitch my idea. I remember being on the edge of my seat as I flipped through its pages and photos within the plan. I'll never forget the gentleman I was pitching to, I'll call him Mr. D. He said, "Man, you're so excited about this place it makes me excited about it too! Let me take this and see what we can do." And they did a lot. Not only did they hand me a check, they threw me a loan signing party complete with a cake!

With ASW it was different, as I didn't need a huge start-up loan. Frankly, we were still paying off our bankruptcy, so even if I did need a loan, I wouldn't have been allowed to apply for one. Starting a writing business, there were small operational fees, very low overhead. I had just enough small jobs to cover my minimal expenses, and I was able to build the business from there.

Stats and Stuff You Need to Know

Banks aren't the only places to find money for your business. Believe it or not, there are a lot of different organizations and individuals out there just looking for the right place to invest their money. The first place of course, for entrepreneurs starting up ventures for the first time, is with close family and friends. Many cafés and service operations get started with personal, private investors. Let's say you need $50,000 to open a bistro. It can be as simple as getting two private loans in the amount of $25,000 each from Grandpa and Aunt Gladys, or as complex as twenty people coughing up $2500 a piece. Make sure these business helpers are in a position to lose what they lend, and don't take money from someone you've had a rocky history with.

Angel investors are affluent individuals who are savvy in the world of entrepreneurs and are looking for just the right budding entrepreneur to invest in. Angels are not usually people you know, but it wouldn't hurt to have a reference or two behind you who they do know, or make sure you have a strong platform in place. Often angel investors are entrepreneurs themselves, and good ones at that. They are worth a try and seem less scary then venture capitalists. Who would be afraid to ask an angel for anything?

Venture capitalists (VCs) are in a league of their own. They are another option for funding your business, especially if your company is of the computer, medical or otherwise techie field. VCs look for ground breaking ideas that will net them big returns. They are interested in companies with a high potential for growth, and may want to come on board a bit later when the company they are investing in has proven itself, and is looking for expansion. VC's like companies that are a sure thing. When doing your homework on VC companies, be sure to take a look at the types of companies they are interested in to see if yours fits. It's not unlike finding a book publisher. There are thousands of publishers out there, but they all publish topics in different genres. For example, I wouldn't submit a romance novel to a text book publisher. The same is true when seeking out a venture capitalist.

Remember when I said you shouldn't be afraid of the IRS? Well the only statement I can make that might surprise you more is this one: Uncle Sam is one of the distant relatives on your contact list most willing to help you get started. What? The Small Business Administration or SBA.gov is by far the best resource for an array of different financing options. They offer loan program guidelines with financial institutions to make getting bank loans a bit easier. The SBA has its own venture capitalist program called the Small Business Investment Company, or SBIC. There is a surety bond program for contractor help and an entire list of "Special Audience" financial assistance programs. These are for borrowers who meet specific requirements, such as veterans, Native Americans, young entrepreneurs and *women*. In fact, the SBA has its own Office of Women's Business Ownership Entrepreneurial Development. There is a mountain of information and resources from the U.S. government, and State government as well. After checking out the national site, check SBA listings within your state.

Speaking of resources specifically for women, there are hundreds of privately funded organizations who give grants and scholarships to help women in business, but there are a lot of scams out there too. Be sure to check, check and triple-check. Use the Better Business Bureau. A woman scorned is likely to lodge a complaint. Ask the grantor for references. Private loans and grants require a lot of time and paperwork make sure all of the effort is going to help you in the long run.

While researching this topic I came across a website that I love, love, love! It is womanowned.com. It is a gold mine for information for women starting their own businesses. When it comes to financing your start-up, they walk you through the process step by step, beginning with checking to make sure your business idea is really a marketable one, and ending with a direct link to who to ask for money. I was so impressed with this website, I applied for membership myself!

Another and perhaps, most obvious type of funding I haven't yet mentioned, is credit cards. Ick. You know how you have been paying for Christmas two years ago on your card because your monthly minimum only covers interest? Imagine doing that with your business. It will not feel good to still be paying for child care equipment that you got rid of six months ago because it was already too worn out to be used safely. The truth is, if you are sure you have the cash flow to pay off your credit card loans every month, go for it. For many start-up businesses, it just isn't the case and they find themselves buried in plastic debt with outrageously high interest rates.

Why This Step (Finding Money) Is So Important

You've heard it before. You've got to spend money to make money. It's a fact. Even in a service business like mine, writing for people, I have to pay for my materials and the electricity to power up my computer. A tailor still needs thread; at the very least you'll have a phone bill.

Surprises will happen. Remember my $30,000 sink fiasco? Be sure to have a little reserve so when something breaks or there is an administrative fee you weren't expecting, you won't have to stop the shop. Take a florist for instance who is just starting out and only has one delivery vehicle and the brakes go out. What is she going to do, tell her client she can't deliver a sympathy wreath to the funeral home? Of course not, that would be a sure way to negate the idea of a return customer. If you can't deliver, in every sense of the word, your customer won't be back. Keep cash on hand for little business emergencies. Money does indeed make the world go 'round, so make sure your business keeps operating within it.

Take Action TODAY

(twenty minutes to an hour each)

1. Make a list of all possible sources of money: close family, friends, angel investors, VC's, banks and private grant organizations
2. Start making calls to lenders and set up meetings. Make sure you have your calendar on hand to keep your schedule straight. Feel free to use the form below to keep track of where your business plan is.
3. When you call your prospective lenders, be sure and ask for the name of the person you will be pitching to. Write a brief cover letter addressed to that person and submit it with your business plan.

Business Plan Tracker

Location of business plan:____________________________

Date it was received/pitched at the above location:

____

Name of contact person:______________________________

Phone and e-mail of contact person:___________________

Follow-up date:______________________________________

Practical Advice

Your idea. Your pet project. Your baby. You know your proposed business better than anyone else. You've done so much research there isn't a question you can't answer. You sit up straighter when you talk about it, your eyes light up and your heart beats faster. You exude confidence. You've practiced your pitch with friends and family, in the mirror and to your dog. Now it is time to pitch it to the moneyman/woman. Whether it is a banker, VC or great Aunt Alice, it is time to fire up your business plan and convey it in such a way that those listening to you get fired up too. You want them to see the same potential as you do. Most importantly, they need to see how investing their money in your project is going to benefit *them*. The banks need to know you'll not only pay off your business loan on time, but when it's time to expand, you will stay loyal and borrow from them again. The venture capitalist wants assurance of a big return in a fairly short amount of time. Even great Aunt Alice wants her money back, perhaps with interest, and at the very least the guarantee you'll name a sandwich after her!

This is the time to sell your business and yourself. If you are at all like me, you hate hard selling. You are probably convinced you are no good at it. I was having lunch with one of my mentors, David R., and I remember telling him how awful I was at sales. He was quick to remind me how I had "sold" the idea of Beanstalks every time I talked about it. It's just that I was so passionate about something I was doing there, some author visit or charity idea, that I was selling it without even knowing I was selling it. There is nothing I dislike more than feeling like I am coercing or pushing someone into something. It is the reason why I do not like cold calls, knocking on doors for politicians, or why I am not an investigative reporter. I just don't like being pushy or nosy or asking too much of anyone. Ah, but pitching your business idea is not like selling raffle tickets or asking for votes. It is about expressing your genuine enthusiasm for your product. It is about telling your story and creating a vision so clear, those listening are compelled to ask for more, and get emotionally drawn in. They will *want* to be a part of what you are planning. Your goal is to not even have to ask, but to have your listener make the first move. When this happens you are selling without selling.

Here is a perfect example of a woman I know who is so passionate about her business that she compelled me, who hates to sell, to want to sell her products. Meet Darby K. She is in the health and wellness business, and sells a line of vegan health and beauty products and cosmetics. She uses the products, and feels and looks fabulous (note Step Nine on Image). She is knowledgeable about the ingredients of her products and the benefits they provide. She practically glows when she is talking about her business, and her people skills are top-notch. Most importantly, she is sincere in her belief that her products are what make the world a better place (don't you want to buy her products already, just by reading this and not even knowing what they are?). Not once did Darby "hard sell" me. Not once did she tell me I should sell her products. Not once was I pressured by her. I met with Darby, I tried the products, and I met with Darby again. Before I knew it, I was part of her team and I hate to sell! *She never even had to ask me.* In fact, I'd probably still be on her team if my writing career hadn't picked up. Now I'm just one of her many satisfied customers. Darby K. is building her future picture, and I try and think of her each time I am pitching one of my ideas. She is sincere and passionate about her product, the two essential elements to a successful pitch. (By the way, if you want to find out more about her awesome product line, I mention it in the acknowledgements.)

Feed Your Energy

Remember, you must act now the way you see yourself in your future picture. You want funding for your business? Start acting like you already have it. What will you do first, once you receive your check? Who will you call? What needs to be purchased? Make your list as if your business account is already fat. By doing this you are playing right into your future picture, feeding your subconscious with positive energy. This keeps you energized and focused on what *will* be.

List the first ten things you will purchase/ when you receive your business funding:

1. ____

2. ____

3. ____

4. ____

5. ____

6. ____

7. ____

8. ____

9. ____

10. ____

Spin It- Turning Negative to Positive

What will you do if the moneyman/woman says no? You go right back to what you've learned about obstacles. What are obstacles? I'm sure you can say it with me by now, obstacles are stepping stones. They are necessary steps to the next great thing. How do we turn obstacles into stepping stones? Ask why the loan/grant was rejected, then use that knowledge to make any necessary changes. For example, in my first business plan, I wanted to be able to pay two managers $30,000 per year. When the bank told me they didn't think this was realistic, I considered my options. Did I need two managers? Did they need to be full time or part-time? Did their duties require the hourly wage I was suggesting? Listen to your obstacle. Make necessary changes and keep moving forward one stepping stone at a time.

Step Eleven: Finding Money Summary

- Remember my story, don't take no for an answer unless you get something from it that moves you forward.
- Research and decide which sources of funding you will seek.
- It takes money to make money.
- Practice your pitch, sell your passion.
- Act as though you already have the money.
- Turn obstacles into stepping stones.

April's Upwords # 1

What are you waiting for? Go! Be that person you've always wanted to be.

In Summary: Cheers

Remember my rock, the one on my desk that reads, "It is time to start living the life you've imagined"? Well, it is *your* time and I, for one, am very excited for you. Loss is tough, no doubt about it. But even at a time when you are at your absolute lowest, there is a reason to look positively ahead, to create your future picture. Not only do I believe this to be true, but this book is a product of this very principal. Failure and success are both matters of interpretation. As a matter of fact, just about everything we do in business is left to interpretation. We choose how we react to customers by how we interpret their concerns, we decide how to handle employees by interpreting their performance, and we analyze every bit of information that comes at us during a routine day of business. Every day has moments of failure or success and is chock full of teaching moments. Don't ignore them. As you've read, my interpretation of these moments is to find a way to see them, always, on an upside. Again, obstacles are stepping stones. They are the necessary steps to the next great thing.

Don't stop seeking, trying and learning because what you've tried in the past didn't work. You took a risk and experienced the loss.

Remember, risk is an important factor toward success. You can choose to fear it and its consequences, dwelling on the what-ifs and catastrophes you've already determined will follow. Or, you can be empowered by it, use it to fuel your determination and leverage yourself to move beyond it.

I have been where you are. It's amazing the strength that is created within us as we learn from our struggles. Remember my favorite quote from Erin Gruwell? A Toast For Change?

"From this moment on, every voice that told you 'you can't' is silenced. Every reason that tells you things will never change disappears. And the person you were before this moment, that person's turn is over. Now it's your turn." --Erin Gruwell

Take a minute to read this quote whenever you are feeling discouraged. You are smart, capable and strong. You have the tools of mindset, due credit, self care, reorganization, dreaming, planning, networking, building platform and image, finding support systems and money. Please use this book as a resource. Go back and look at all of the lists you have made and the notes you've taken, and update them as you move through your new venture. No matter what stage you are experiencing at this moment, whether you are still on your couch or cashing your new business loan check, you must know that every little action leads to another and another, and will eventually be your next great thing.

Here is to you getting off your couch, and embracing the starring role of your own future picture. Cheers!

Glossary of Terms

Action Learning—an educational process where people study their own actions and experiences in order to improve performance, developed by Reginald Revans in the 1940's

Angel Investor—affluent individuals looking for just the right budding entrepreneur to invest in

Balance Sheet—financial statement for a specific date showing both assets and claims

Bankruptcy Chapter 7—a court appointed trustee liquefies assets/distributes proceeds to creditors

Bankruptcy Chapter 11—allows the business to reorganize and rehabilitate, and use the restructuring to pay off debt from future earnings

Bankruptcy Chapter 13—a structured repayment plan monitored by a court appointed trustee

Break Even Analysis—the estimation of the point when profits clear debt

Cash Flow—after tax profit plus non-cash dues and depreciation

Cold Call—a sales call to a complete stranger

Cork Exercise*-an enunciation exercise to help loosen facial muscles by talking with a cork held between your front teeth

Creditor—an individual or company owed money

Demographics—information/data about a particular population

Energy—the feeling or aura around a person, often positive or negative

Executive Summary—the main points/overview of a business plan

Future Picture*-a "movie in your head" where you see yourself having achieved your ultimate goals

Hard Sell—a direct sales pitch with no hidden agenda or subtleties

Idea Map—a visual expression of thought processes

Idea Mapping—a whole-brained thinking tool that enhances memory, thought organization, planning, creativity and communication

Image—the way one is perceived; carries them self

Legal Entity—the organization of a business either by sole proprietorship, partnership, S-corp or C-corp

Market Comparison—a side by side comparison between one's business and direct competition

Mentor—a trusted, influential, more experienced or senior counselor

Mindset—the attitude in which one is driven

Mom Factor*-the desire to take care of one's self to assure the caring for of others

Networking—in business, meeting and seeking colleagues and referrals

Next Great Thing*-one's next main goal

Obstacles*-detours of one's path, overcome by learned knowledge. O/LK=SS (obstacles divided by learned knowledge equals stepping stones)

Personal Brand—one's own image as projected to the public

Personal Guarantee—a financial agreement allowing a defaulted financial institution to take action for collection against both business and personal assets

Pitch—a summation of a proposition or idea

Platform—a personal brand, giving one more visibility in their field

Positive Knowing*--believing with emotion a goal has been reached, even before it actually has

Positive Psychology—the study of healthy mindedness which explores the optimal functioning of people/groups

Positive Thinking—putting a positive spin on any situation, optimism

Profit & Loss—gain and loss from business transactions as reported in bookkeeping

PTA—Parent Teacher Association, a non-profit volunteer organization of parents with children in school and teachers. PTO is the same thing. It stands for Parent Teacher Organization.

Public Relations Agencies—agencies which obtain publicity for an individual/business/group for a fee

Sales Forecast—an estimate of future sales based on evidence

SBA—Small Business Administration, a government organization that aids entrepreneurs and small business owners

SBIC—Small Business Investment Company, a government venture capitalist program

SCORE—a non-profit organization offering free, confidential counseling for small business, made up of retired executives

SEO—Search Engine Optimization, a use of wordage in web content easily recognized by search engines

SLI—Saline Leadership Institute, a year -long curriculum focusing on leadership and community relations/involvement in Saline, Michigan

SWOT Analysis—a business tool using information from one's Strengths, Weaknesses, Opportunities and Threats

Venture Capitalist—investment companies that financially support companies with high growth potential, and expect a high return for their investment

Vision Board—a tool to help one visualize his/her future picture, ultimate goals

Voice Quality—how pleasing the voice is to listen to

*as defined/created by April Scarlett

Sources

Advani, Asheesh. "Using Credit Cards to Fund Your Business." *entrepreneur.com* n. pag. Web. 2 Apr 2011. <http://www.entrepreneur.com/article/81822"www.entrepreneur.com/article/81822>.

Advani, Asheesh. "Deciding Whom To Ask For Money." *entrepreneur.com* n. pag. Web. 2 Apr 2011. <www.entrepreneur.com/article/83792>.

"business-relationships-how-to-create-and-keep-relationships." *buzzle.com*. N.p., n.d. Web. 2 Apr 2011. <http://www.buzzle.com/articles/building-business-relationships.html"www.buzzle.com/articles/building-business-relationships-how-to-create-and-keep-relationships.html>

Framingham Ph. D, Jane. "The Power of Positive Thinking." *psychcentral.com* (2006): n. pag. Web. 2 Apr 2011. <www.psychcentral.com/lib/2006/the-power-of-positive-thingking.html >.

Fry, Richard. "Minorities and the Recession-Era Enrollment Boom." *Pew Research Center* (2010) n. pag. Web. 2 Apr 2011.

Gable, Shelly L. . "Review of General Psychology." *Review of General Psychology* 9.2 (2005): 103-110 . Web. 2 Apr 2011.

www.gaebler.com/small-business-bankruptcy.htm

Goode, Eric. "Power of Positive Thinking May Have a Health Benefit, Study says." *nytimes.com* (2003): n. pag. Web. 2 Apr 2011.

Gordon, Kim T. "7 Relationship-Building Strategies for Your Business." *entrepreneur.com* n. pag. Web. 2 Apr 2011. <www. Entrepreneur.com/article/66228 >.

Gruwell, Erin, Freedom Writers Foundation

Schuchi, Kaira. "The Power of Positive Thinking: The Key To Health and Happiness." *brighthub.com* n. pag. Web. 2 Apr 2011. <www.brighthub.com/health/alternative-medicine/articles/36221>.

Koerth-Baker, Maggie. "The Power of Positive Thinking: Truth or Myth?." *livescience.com* n. pag. Web. 2 Apr 2011. <www.livescience.com/health/080829-happy-thoughts.html>.

Knutson, VanCauter. "Association Between Sleep and Blood Pressure In Midlife." *Arch Intern* 169.11 (2009): n. pag. Web. 2 Apr 2011. Rathouz, Yan, Hulley, Liu, Lauderdale

Krotz, Joanna L. "Get Results From a PR Firm." *microsoft.com* n. pag. Web. 2 Apr 2011. <www.microsoft.com/business/en-us/resources/ArticleReader.htm >.

Leadinginsights.com

Lonerangerart.com

Moranlaw.net

Nast, Jamie. *Idea Mapping Success*. Jamie Nast, Web. 3 Apr 2011. <http://www.ideamappingsuccess.com/"www.ideamappingsuccess.com>.

Office of Health Education and Promotion. UNH Health Services, Web. 3 Apr 2011.

O'Neill, Sorhaindo. "Negative Health Effects of Financial Stress." *Consumer Interests Annual* 51. (2005): n. pag. Web. 3 Apr 2011.

_N.p., n.d. Web. 3 Apr 2011. <http://www.personalfinancefoundation.org/"www.personalfinancefoundation.org>.

_N.p., n.d. Web. 3 Apr 2011. <http://www.smallbiztrends.com/2010/10/building-business-relationships.html"www.smallbiztrends.com/2010/10/building-business-relationships.html>.

"Positive Thinking" A Spoonful of Optimism." n. pag. Web. 3 Apr 2011. <"http://www.,independent.co.uk/lifestyle/health-and-families"www..independent.co.uk/lifestyle/health-and-families.htm>.

Reigh, Marlena. *yourvoicesuccess.com*. Web. 3 Apr 2011. <http://www.yourvoicesuccess.com/"www.yourvoicesuccess.com>.

"Small Business Survival Rates." *score.org*. N.p., n.d. Web. 3 Apr 2011.

Stibich Ph.D, Mark. "Tips For Great Naps." *longevity.about.com*. about.com, Web. 3 Apr 2011. <http://www.longevity.about.com/ed/sleep/a/napping_tips.htm"www.longevity.about.com/ed/sleep/a/napping_tips.htm >.

Torres, Nicole. "Joining a Support Group." *entrepreneur.com* n. pag. Web. 3 Apr 2011. <www.entrepreneur.com/article/45002>.

University of Louisville. N.p., n.d. Web. 3 Apr 2011. <http://www.louisville.edu/web/behavioraloncology/research-projects/research"www.louisville.edu/web/behavioraloncology/research-projects/research>.

_N.p., n.d. Web. 3 Apr 2011. <http://www.uscourts.gov/FederalCourts/Bankruptcy/BankruptcyBasics/Chapter13.aspx"www.uscourts.gov/FederalCourts/Bankruptcy/BankruptcyBasics/Chapter13.aspx>.

More Resources

American Business Women's Association

April Scarlett Motherboard

April Scarlett Sports For Chicks

April Scarlett Writes

Arbonne.com (Darby Kolano)

Emily's List

National Organization For Women, now.org

Woman Owned, womenowned.org

Positively April Scarlett

Small Business Administration, sba.gov

Successful Women Weekly

Women On Business.com

FOR HELP WITH DOMESTIC VIOLENCE

thehotline.org (includes a "quick exit" button to leave the site in a hurry), 1-800-799-SAFE (7233), TTY 1-800-787-3224

Safehorizon.org, 1-800-621- HOPE (4673)

Acknowledgements and About the Author

Acknowledgements

This project was born out of the kind of life changing trial, which at first glance had the power to discourage and ruin. Instead, thanks to so many, it has opened doors, and keeps leading me in such exciting directions, that I find myself grateful for the trial in the first place.

First of all there wouldn't be a book in hand if not for David R. Haslam and the team at HMSI Publishing. David and I hit it off immediately, and his guidance, insight into the publishing world, and patience with my lack thereof are appreciated. Before the manuscript reached the hands of HMSI, however, it was scoured over, directed and re-directed, talked through and streamlined by my editor, who is also my awesome brother, Geoffrey Bankowski. Despite his busy schedule teaching, editing, writing, and producing music for his band (Good and Angry in Brooklyn, NY--shameless plug), he always made time for me, and still does. And finally, while in the hands of HMSI editors, I looked to my early readers. These were the only people to whom I handed over my manuscript for critique and opinion. Thank you James Scarlett (more about him later), Monique Castria, Jamie Nast and Patty Williamson.

You'll notice the photo on the back....I so like black and white prints! Thank you Lorissa Farr (photosbylorissa.com) for making the best of a very windy, rainy day. My cut and color are always done by the fabulous Stephanie Celkis, and make-up for my special events is done by Darby Kolano (arbonne.com). Thanks ladies!

My story in this book starts with Beanstalks, so thank you to my customers, employees, landlords and the business community in Saline who supported me as a brick and mortar. This includes the Saline Area Chamber of Commerce, the City of Saline, the Saline Downtown Merchants Association, mentors David Rhoads and Art Trapp, and my fellow merchants downtown. One shout out especially to Paul Geragosian at Brecon Grille. Whenever there is a chance to promote my brand, then and now, he is the first to say "yes!" Thank you Paul for your support and for the use of your terrific restaurant for the book release party.

My return to writing meant sending out stories wherever I could, and Michelle Rogers at the Saline Reporter was the first one to give me a shot. One feature led to another and another. Thanks Michelle for letting me re-wet my writing feet. Thanks to other publications that continually accept my work and assign new stuff: Patch.com, Heritage News, and annarbor.com (blogs), and all of my commercial and freelance clients. Thanks to each of you, I was confident enough to write this book.

Thanks to all of my readers: blog readers, Facebook fans (likers!), Twitter followers and owners of this book. I have pins for each of you on my world map. It is so amazing to believe I have readers on five continents.

A special mention to Tony Dixon and the gang at A2YP.TV, and Dark Elf Entertainment for giving me the opportunity to expand my brand. I am so happy to know and work with all of you!

Thanks to women in business who inspire me, and to family and friends who support me. A special thanks to all of the Pleasant Ridge moms who are now my good friends. You gave me a "place" to fit in after Beanstalks fell apart. I'm so excited to continue on with all of you as our children grow and move on too.

A quick meow to our cat, Ringo. I know, I know, give me a break...but he has kept me company while I write, sitting atop my desk, listening to me read aloud or talk to myself, when the rest of the family slept or were away at work and school.

And finally...I must talk about the men in my life. James, love of my life and biggest cheerleader on the planet. As I've mentioned in this book, your support has been unwavering. Everywhere you go, you pump me up to everyone you know. You are truly a dream of a partner in life, and every other endeavor we find ourselves in. Stone, my oldest son, a teen beyond your years. You read my stuff, believe in my optimism, try and keep me up with the times, and make me a proud and confident parent. You've always got my back, and now the strength and muscles to back it up...LOL. Keep writing too, son. Your fiction is better than mine! And Samuel, my witty and charming heart. Your hugs, sense of wonder and contagious laughter fuel me on a daily basis. You are in so many of my stories, because you come from such a place of imagination and possibility. I am so lucky to have the three of you in my life each and every day. It is because of you, my men, that I am inspired to succeed with everything that I do. We four.

April Scarlett
Saline, Michigan, USA
April, 2011

About the Author

April Scarlett is a freelance writer, author and media personality. She authors five blogs and writes for local and regional news publications, as well as for the magazine and juvenile markets. Her passion however, is finding just the right words to uplift and empower women, especially the ones who don't even know they've got gifts to share! April's favorite phrase, "It's time to start living the life you've imagined," is her mantra. "There is nothing I like more than to be able to help a woman, especially after she's faced a setback or challenge, to get back to reaching for her dream, or perhaps help her find a new one."

April, herself, knows just what it is like to bounce back from setback. It was in 2009 when she lost her business to the recession, and in turn lost everything else, including her home. It was at her lowest point when she was able to see that the loss of her business was not an obstacle, but merely a stepping stone to her next great thing. Now April spends her time writing about ways to help others who are going through the same thing!

When April is not writing, she is the host of "*The Business Spotlight*", an internet television program for WDEE.TV. With an extensive background in radio, internet television is an easy fit. She returns to the radio airwaves twice a year to WSDP, where she helps out with their pledge drives and alumni weekends. April also fills in from time to time as an on-air moderator for a weekly spot featuring the local Chamber of Commerce.

April is most happy when spending time with her family. She is married to Jim Scarlett and mom to sons Stone and Sam. Her boys keep her very busy with school, football, wrestling, basketball and chess and show choir! She loves life with her family in Saline, MI where she is very involved within her community, schools and City. She sits on two Boards of Directors and gets involved with as many community projects as will fit her schedule.

April is pursuing her degree in Professional Communications, and is certified by the Institute of Children's Literature. She also attended the American Academy of Dramatic Arts in Pasadena, CA and is a graduate of the Saline Leadership Institute.

For access to all of April's work, please visit www.aprilscarlett.com .

Breinigsville, PA USA
13 April 2011
259741BV00004B/1/P

9 780982 694572